Twayne's English Authors Series

Sylvia E. Bowman, *Editor*

INDIANA UNIVERSITY

H. G. Wells

(TEAS) 43

H. G. Wells

By RICHARD HAUER COSTA

Utica College of Syracuse University

Twayne Publishers, Inc.   ::   New York

MANUFACTURED IN THE UNITED STATES OF AMERICA

For Jo

"Of the vast and diversified library he left us, nothing has pleased me more than his narration of some atrocious miracles: *The Time Machine, The Island of Dr. Moreau, The First Men in the Moon.* They are the first books I read; perhaps they will be the last. I think they will be incorporated, like the fables of Theseus or Ahasuerus, into the general memory of the species and even transcend the fame of their creator or the extinction of the language in which they were written."

—Jorge Luis Borges

Preface

Although acknowledging with Professor W. Warren Wagar, today's foremost Wellsian, that it is impossible to try to make H. G. Wells into a conventional man of letters, this book resists any tendency to treat him as other than a literary figure of almost the first order.

For more than a generation it has been fashionable for critics to accept Wells wholly on his own terms; to take to heart his last words to Henry James about his preference for being journalist over artist; and to remember only the image presented by his long eunuch period, the last thirty years of an intensely productive life. That picture of world-state trumpeter invoking mankind to follow his lead to a promised land provided a convenient scapegoat for other voices in the deepening shadow of World War II. It drew the scoffing of literati of existential bent who were coming of age even as the aging seer tried to hard-sell the world a hope that his earliest and best books could not support.

The flaw of contemporary criticism is in its totemizing of the public Wells—educator, publicist, blue-printer of utopia—and its neglect of the Wells who will live: the creator of a major Edwardian trilogy and at least five scientific romances which are Swiftian in their mythopoeic brilliance. The major aim of this book is, therefore, to show that the Wells who will live is the Wells of science-fiction-esque fantasy and exuberant comic novels in the vein of Dickens. A corollary aim is to demonstrate that the teaching and preaching Wells engaged in a spiritual Armageddon with the authentic Wells. The struggle produced a state of war between the public celebrity and the private artist. It was a battle whose wounds soiled novel after novel in Wells's last three decades.

The first six chapters are about the Wells who will live. Without a close view of Wells's first thirty years, no student can fully grasp the rightness of Richard Rees's contention that Wells was the first "angry young man" in English literature. Chapter One, which tells the "angry young man's" story, is drawn about equally from Well's life-novels and the pages of his autobiography. Chapter Two seeks to place him generally as a major writer of fiction. Chapters Three through Six deal in detail with the products of Wells's golden period, 1895–1910.

Chapters Seven through Nine try to place in a non-specialist way the by-products of the artist's life. These works were the output of H. G. Wells's other lives: sociological-political novelist; Fabian and feminist (Chapter Seven); misled advocate of the novel of ideas in losing conflict with Henry James (Chapter Eight); and utopographer and world statesman (Chapter Nine). The utopian and historian roles obliged Wells to wear hats that ill-fitted him. To assess Wells's contribution in these two areas is, therefore, beyond the province of this book. For the best study of the eclectic Wells, I urge the reading of Professor Wagar's superb work on the man of ideas, *H. G. Wells and the World State.*

Chapter Ten focuses on the book's recurrent theme—the one ably espoused by Wells's son, Anthony West—that the apparently abrupt misanthropy of H. G. W.'s last years was actually a return to the dark skepticism of his most creative period: a return to a spiritual country he had never left.

The final chapter urges a full reappraisal of one of this century's most representative, if misunderstood, writers.

Richard Hauer Costa

Utica, N. Y.

Acknowledgments

For permission to quote some thirty of the works of H. G. Wells I am indebted to the executors of his estate, his sons, Dr. G. P. Wells, University College London, and Frank Wells.

For permission to quote from the following works, I am indebted to these writers and publishers: Vincent Brome, *H. G. Wells*, Longmans, Green & Co.; Bernard Bergonzi, *The Early H. G. Wells*, University of Toronto; Leon Edel and Gordon N. Ray, eds., *Henry James and H. G. Wells*, University of Illinois; Norman Nicholson, *H. G. Wells*, Alan Swallow; W. Warren Wagar, *H. G. Wells and the World State*, Yale University; Anthony West, "The Dark World of H. G. Wells," Harper's Magazine.

I can merely record, though never adequately express, my gratitude to Edmund Wilson who, through an accident of geography, made his summer home and his presence available to me for a number of fruitful discussions of the influence of Wells on his (Wilson's) generation.

I should like to acknowledge two cases of special indebtedness: to Mark R. Hillegas who through another accident of geography —Colgate University and Utica College are within an hour's drive of each other—made his profound knowledge of Wells's scientific romances accessible to me; and to John F. Hopkins, as head of the Fiction Department, Free Library of Philadelphia, and a personal friend for twenty-five years, who guided me into many a Wellsian path I might never have found.

To Gordon N. Ray and Royal Gettmann my special thanks are due for permission to use the valuable materials of the H. G. Wells Archive, University of Illinois at Urbana, in the summer of 1962. I am also indebted to Mary Dudley and her staff at the Utica College library for painstaking efforts to obtain materials on microfilm and inter-library loan; to the library staffs of Hamilton College, Colgate University, and Syracuse University for their cooperation.

I am indebted also to Thomas F. O'Donnell and Raymond Simon, chairmen of Languages and Business Administration, respectively, at Utica College of Syracuse University for their forbearance over the long haul; to two of my teachers, Mary Elizabeth Clark, who made H. G. Wells required reading in her modern novel class, and Roland E. Wolseley, who first encouraged me to apply my interest in Wells to a book.

I should like to thank Utica College for grants which helped to free me to work on the book.

I should like to thank Dorothy Judd Sickels, chairman of publications at Utica College, for her generous assistance in preparing the galley and page proofs.

And finally I should like to acknowledge my indebtedness to Sylvia E. Bowman and Robert J. Milch, the copy-editor at Twayne, for intelligent and conscientious editorial supervision.

Contents

Chronology

1866   Herbert George Wells born September 21 at Bromley in Kent, England, to Joseph Wells and Sarah Neal Wells; two older brothers, Frank and Fred.

1874   Broke leg in fall. Turned to books for first time. Long convalescence to develop reading habit later seen by Wells as significant in struggle to escape lower middle-class origins.

1874–   Attended Thomas Morley's Commercial Academy.
1880

1880   Mother became housekeeper at Up Park, manor house of Sir Harry Featherstonhaugh, and took Herbert George with her. Reading broadened with availability of books in quantity.

1881   Failed as pharmacist's apprentice; sent local Grammar School as boarder pupil; apprenticed as assistant in drapery shop.

1883   Ran away from drapery shop; became teacher in preparatory school.

1884–   Student at Normal School of Science, London; studied
1887   biology under Thomas H. Huxley.

1887   Health broken; found to have damaged kidney and tendency to be consumptive.

1888   Published serially first considerable literary work, the unfinished *Chronic Argonauts*, in *The Science Schools Journal;* it was early version of *The Time Machine.*

1891   October, married Isabell Mary Wells, a cousin. Essay, "The Rediscovery of the Unique," accepted by Frank Harris and published in *The Fortnightly Review;* considered serious start of literary career.

1893   Met Amy Catherine Robbins while tutoring her in biology. Suffered physical breakdown forcing him to abandon teaching forever; determined to pursue literary career.

1895   Published *The Time Machine* to instant acclaim; also, *Select Conversations with an Uncle, The Stolen Bacillus and other Incidents,* and *The Wonderful Visit.* Divorced by Isabel Mary Wells; married Amy Catherine Robbins. Met George Bernard Shaw.

1896   *The Island of Dr. Moreau* and *The Wheels of Chance* published. Formed close friendships with George Gissing, Arnold Bennett, Henry James, Joseph Conrad, and other fellow novelists.

1897   *The Plattner Story and Others, The Invisible Man,* and *Thirty Strange Stories.*

1898   *The War of the Worlds.*

1899   *When the Sleeper Awakes.*

1900   *Love and Mr. Lewisham.*

1901   *Anticipations* and *The First Men in the Moon.* Son, George Philip Wells, born.

1902   *The Sea Lady.*

1903   *Mankind in the Making* and *Twelve Stories and a Dream.*

Second son, Frank Richard Wells, born. Rushed to bedside of George Gissing just before his death in south of France. Joined Fabian Society; gave first public lecture before Fabians.

1904   *The Food of the Gods.*

1905   *A Modern Utopia* and *Kipps.* His mother, Sarah Wells, died.

1906   *In the Days of the Comet.* Engaged in year-long factional struggle within Fabians in which he was defeated by old-guard led by Shaw.

1907   *First and Last Things.*

1908   *New Worlds for Old* and *The War in the Air.* Resigned from the Fabian Society.

1909   *Tono-Bungay* and *Ann Veronica.*

1910   *The History of Mr. Polly.* His father, Joseph Wells, died.

1911   *The New Machiavelli.* Wrote essay in *Fortnightly Review* expressing his intention of expanding scope of the novel to include ideas. *The Country of the Blind, and Other Stories,* including all stories he thought to have merit, published.

1912   *Marriage.*

1913   *The Passionate Friends.*

1914   Made first visit to Russia. *The World Set Free,* containing forecast of atomic warfare, published. Also published *The War That Will End War,* an optimistic forecast of the outcome of the great war. *The Wife of Sir Isaac Harman.* Son, Anthony West, born to Cicely Fairfield (Rebecca West) and Wells, August 5.

1915 *Boon* published, touching off bitter exchange of letters with Henry James, whose attitude toward the novel was parodied in this book. *The Research Magnificent.*

1916 *Mr. Britling Sees It Through* published; became an immediate best-seller in both England and the United States. Visited Italian, French and German fronts.

1917 *God the Invisible King* and *The Soul of a Bishop.*

1918 Advocated League of Free Nations as requisite to gaining permanent peace. Published *In the Fourth Year* and *Joan and Peter.* Collaborated with others in preparing propaganda literature against Germany.

1919 Resigned from the League of Nations Union. Decided to write a comprehensive world history; embarked on *The Outline of History. The Undying Fire* published.

1920 Second visit to Russia; talked to Lenin. *Russia in the Shadows* published. *The Outline of History* published; sold quarter of a million copies in first American edition.

1921 Modernized dramatic version of *The Wonderful Visit* performed in London. Accepted invitation of the *New York World* to cover Washington peace conference as special correspondent. Referred to by Anatole France in an interview as the most intelligent of the English. *The Salvaging of Civilization* published.

1922 Became member of Labor Party; accepted Labor candidacy for the Lord Rectorship of Glasgow University but was defeated; defeated in bid for Parliament. *The Secret Places of the Heart* published.

1923 *Men Like Gods.*

1924 Atlantic Edition of his works published in twenty-eight volumes. *The Story of a Great Schoolmaster* and *The Dream* published.

1925   *Christina Alberta's Father.*

1926   *The World of William Clissold.*

1927   Wife, Amy Catherine Wells, died. *Meanwhile* published. Began collaboration with Julian Huxley and his son, G. P. Wells, on a major outline of biology.

1928   Arranged for publication of *The Book of Catherine Wells,* containing the writings of his late wife. *Mr. Blettsworthy on Rampole Island* published.

1929   *The King Who Was a King.*

1930   *The Autocracy of Mr. Parham* and *The Science of Life.*

1932   *The Work, Wealth and Happiness of Mankind.*

1933   *The Shape of Things to Come.*

1934   Made third visit to Russia for talk with Stalin. Entered into public controversy with Shaw over the Kremlin interview. Visited the United States for talk with President Franklin D. Roosevelt. *Experiment in Autobiography* published.

1935   Wrote film scenarios for *Things to Come* and *The Man Who Could Work Miracles.*

1936   *The Anatomy of Frustration* and *The Croquet Player.* Banquet celebrating seventieth birthday attended by hundreds.

1937   *Brynhild* and *Star-Begotten.*

1938   *Apropos of Dolores* published. Orson Welles's radio broadcast, based on War of the Worlds, frightens much of the United States.

1939   *The Fate of Homo Sapiens* and *The Holy Terror* published.

1940   *Babes in the Darkling Wood* published. Went to the United States on lecture tour.

1941   *You Can't Be Too Careful* published.

1942   Suffered near-fatal physical collapse, but remained in London throughout the Blitz.

1945   *Mind at the End of Its Tether* published.

1946   Died August 13 in eightieth year.

H. G. Wells

CHAPTER 1

Life and Times

I Pip Without Great Expectations

WHAT is perhaps the most amply self-documented life in the annals of English literature began on September 21, 1866, when to Sarah Neal Wells, a lady's maid, and to Joseph Wells, an unsuccessful tradesman though accomplished cricket-player, was born the last of three sons, Herbert George Wells. The infant first "squinted and bubbled at the universe" in a shabby bedroom over a china shop in Bromley, Kent, that was called "Atlas House." Wells, in the retrospect provided by his massive *Experiment in Autobiography* (1934), appears to have retained a devotion to his parents tempered by his rebel's view of them as victims of the inflexible society into which they were born.

Sarah Wells, viewed almost clinically in the autobiography, committed the one unpardonable sin in her son's cosmology: she had a "set" mind about religion, respectability, and her "place." She took for granted her Victorian world, the one her Bertie was to spend a lifetime exorcizing from his soul. Not even her desperate single-handed battle to keep the family afloat made her sense for a moment that "her God in his Heaven was under notice to quit." But from this little black figure of a woman "curiously suggestive (in later years) of Her Majesty Queen Victoria," [1] Wells inherited an awareness of the impact of a god-figure. If he could not adhere to the furious deity to whom he was compelled to pray as a child, he sensed his need for something to fill the void, a God-substitute, which in his books was to take many names. [2] This need he took from his mother, along with a stoicism that stood him well during a lifetime of bodily ills and during a shattering period when he nursed his devoted wife Jane in what both knew was a futile effort to stave off a fatal disease.

Undistinguished as he was, Joseph Wells evokes poignant recollections from his son in the matchless early pages of the autobiography. Principally, however, Wells views him in the context of a social system he despised: as a not-quite-willing victim of eighteenth-century determinism in which, for such as he, only a chance legacy might offer passage out of the humdrum from cradle to grave. Wells's portrait of Mr. Polly (1910) is a tribute to the man his father might have been, but where Mr. Polly broke out in true Wellsian style from the bondage of circumstance, Herbert George's father reserved his dreams for stargazing, a practice which only affirmed his enslavement. Wells was to write twenty-five years after his father's death that if Joseph Wells "could look out of this planet and wonder about the stars, it may be he could also look out of his immediate circumstances and apprehend their triviality by stellar standards." [3]

If stargazing provided an imaginative springboard which in Bertie Wells would culminate in several of literature's best cosmic voyages, it probably contributed to his father's undoing. At any rate, Joseph Wells was as deficient at shopkeeping as Mr. Polly, and the household in Bromley trembled constantly on the verge of financial collapse. Wells never forgot the shadows of insolvency which threatened Atlas House. At the end of his autobiographical novel, *Tono-Bungay,* published when Wells was forty-three, the enterprising Teddy Ponderevo dies after an over-extended, rags-to-riches venture with a fake patent medicine. Writing in 1915, Van Wyck Brooks, himself a typical new-worlds-for-old Wellsian, saw *Tono-Bungay* as "an epic of irresponsible capitalism from the socialist point of view." [4] But the book and its preposterous (for 1908) Ponderevo are, in a more human sense, a projection from the Victorian point of view by Wells of the doom that awaited solo upstart adventurers.

The student of Victorian life as seen through novels might contrast the below-stairs, teatime-among-servants scene in *Tono-Bungay* with any of Pip's interviews with the aristocratic Miss Havisham in *Great Expectations.* From the gossipy small talk of the pensioned ex-servants who visit the mother of George Ponderevo at Bladesover House, one senses a fear of gentry. In the petty contempt of the hired help for their betters, Wells reveals a rarely articulated detestation of the System. Dickens is less subtle. At the point in *Great Expectations* where Pip suffers the humiliation of presenting his indentures to the doughty Miss Havisham,

Dickens paints decadence in broad strokes. It is felt in Miss Havisham's dusty lace and in the fire which, in approved Victorian-novel style, levels country-houses and caste alike. Only a kind of residue of noblesse oblige keeps Miss Havisham from dissolving in flames before our eyes.

Bladesover in *Tono-Bungay* is, of course, the Up Park of Wells's childhood.[5] It had been there in the 1850's that Sarah Neal met Joseph Wells. She was engaged as a maid on the estate of Sir Henry Featherstonhaugh; the man she was to marry worked as a gardener. Years later, when it became obvious to the mother of three that the failure of Joseph Wells's shop was only a matter of time, she accepted a call to return as a stroke of heavenly fortune. Her other two sons safely apprenticed to drapers, Sarah Wells took her youngest, thirteen-year-old Bertie, with her and became housekeeper at Up Park in 1880.

The change in outlook from a shopkeeper's window to below stairs in a manor house was salutary for the youth. Bertie took more from Sir Harry Featherstonhaugh's fossil of a dying age than the son of a domestic had the right to expect. Not only did the dislocation close, at least temporarily, the almost inevitable path to being a tradesman, but it enabled Bertie to encounter books in profusion for the first time. In the late Sir Harry's library, the boy made the acquaintance of the lucid satire of Voltaire, the unexpurgated *Gulliver*—a reading which established Wells's lifelong debt to Swift—and the liberating air of Plato's *Republic*. Despite the attenuated social life, Wells would one day write of the Up Park days, that life became charged with potency for the house "retained a vitality that altogether overshadowed the insignificant trickle of upstairs life."[6]

But Bertie's deliverance from the fate of his brothers was only temporary. Almost as unquestioning as her belief in God and Savior was Sarah Wells's belief in drapery. From the habit of servility came her conviction that the best of positions for a young man lay in wearing a black coat and tie behind a counter. So the last-born son of Joseph and Sarah Wells was made to put his books away, give up drawing, painting and every sort of free delight, and slip almost unprotestingly into the mold cast for boys of his class. Thrown aside, too, was the boy's first attempt at fiction, the writing and illustrating of a gaily tragic tale, "The Desert

Daisy." [7] Begun shortly before his mother returned to Up Park, it involved an ill-starred romance, a thieving bishop (the clergy never came off well in any of his early work, published or unpublished), and a bloody conflict between the Kingdoms of Spade and Clubs. There was gore and violence—infants hurled at the enemy like projectiles, dismemberment practiced with relish. Thematically, Wells was already cutting his teeth on what would become familiar morsels: the satirization of royalty, government and church, the army, and even—without stinting—himself. The books, those to be read as well as those to be written, were apparently left behind as Bertie Wells, turning fourteen—a Pip without any great expectations—was set down from an uncle's dogcart and apprenticed to a fate proper to his place.

There is little point in tracing his half-dozen or so "starts" in life—to use the word Wells employs in the early pages of his autobiography. His education was desultory and fragmentary, alternating as it did in its adolescent phases with abysmally unhappy periods of apprenticeship, first to drapers and later to dry-goods dealers and druggists. Wells, in a moving segment of *Tono-Bungay,* tells how George Ponderevo—his history showing insubordination, unjust charges of pilferage, and unpopularity wherever he was apprenticed—got up early one Sunday morning and walked nearly twenty miles to Bladesover to proclaim to his mother that the latest drapery experiment had to end.[8]

In the world of tradesmen, Wells learned about the Pollys, Artie Kippses, and Teddy Ponderevos. He came perilously close to living out the life of Mr. Polly, his most lasting creation, without that little man's saving recourse to arson. He might have remained an underpaid science teacher like Mr. Lewisham, with a schema for life that would have included marriage and children, but not a lifelong chafing against convention in a hundred books. He might have had, with his Artie Kipps, only vague intimations of greatness without the pull of literary success that elevated him to a kind of world statesmanship of letters: confrontations with Theodore and Franklin D. Roosevelt, Lenin, Stalin, and most of the other figures who shaped human destiny during the first third of the twentieth century, such as are virtually closed to even the most eminent of today's literati.[9]

H. G. Wells escaped anonymity through a door few men of

letters used before him and only an occasional C. P. Snow has used since. He began to pass examinations and to show unusual ability in science; when he was eighteen, he was offered a scholarship at the Normal School of Science, South Kensington, to train as a teacher.

II *Haven and Huxley*

Wells came to London for the first time in the summer of 1884, an occasion he termed "one of the great days of my life." There he encountered one of his gods, Professor Thomas H. Huxley, who would be his teacher in elementary biology and, later, in zoology. Fifty years later Wells wrote of his study under Huxley, that "it was beyond question the most educational year of my life. It left me under that urgency for coherence and consistency, that repugnance from haphazard assumptions and arbitrary statements, which is the essential distinction of the educated from the uneducated mind." [10]

One can imagine the impact on the young science student, of stories current among the older assistants about times only recently past when Charles Darwin had entered the lecture-auditorium to hear his friend. Darwin had been dead less than two years, and Huxley was still a decade away from delivering his lecture on "Ethics and Evolution" before the University of Oxford.

In a moving passage from his autobiography Wells sees Darwin and Huxley as coevals in the intellectual revolution taking place in the nineteenth century under science's agency: one that was, in Huxley's words, "teaching the world that the ultimate court of appeal is observation and experiment, and not authority. . . ." [11] Wells writes:

Little men will stand on the shoulders of giants to the end of time and small birds foul the nests in which they were hatched. Darwin and Huxley knew about one per cent of the facts about variation and mutation that are accessible to Mr. Whippersnapper. That does not alter the fundamental magnificence of Darwin's and Huxley's achievement. They put the fact of organic evolution upon an impregnable base of proof and demonstration. . . . Darwin and Huxley . . . belong to the same aristocracy as Plato and Aristotle and Galileo, and they will ultimately dominate the priestly and orthodox mind as surely, because there is a response, however reluctant, masked and stifled, in every human soul to rightness and a firmly stated truth. (pp. 162–63)

As early as 1915 Van Wyck Brooks saw the imprint of Huxley on the scientific romances of Wells. Huxley espoused a theory of evolution in which the world and the universe, society and nature, are viewed as operating at cross purposes, with man pitting mind against matter. The only chance for social and ethical progress is the "checking of the cosmic process at every step" and the replacement of it by the ethical. But, as Houston Peterson notes, Huxley has "no fantastic hopes" for the efficacy of man's assault on the cosmos.[12] He sees no necessary millennium, not even a better life on earth, in the theory of evolution. For him, the theory points to a time when the cosmic process will destroy man. If, as Huxley believed, evolution involves a "constant remodeling of the organism in adaptation to new conditions," retrogressive change is both as possible and practicable as progressive. The course of earthly life is like the trajectory of "a ball fired from a mortar," and "the sinking half of that course is as much a part of the general process of evolution as the rising." [13]

The dread potential for destruction held by forces outside man, was gleaned by H. G. Wells in the laboratory and made palpable in those cosmic phenomena so dear to his heart: colliding comets, invading Martians, monstrous creatures seen in the Time Traveller's kaleidoscope of the earth's dying. "It has always been a fixed conviction with Wells that man personal and man social is dancing on a volcano," wrote Brooks[14] at a time when the emergent image of Wells as the jolly apostle of scientific materialism, the forger of new (and invariably better) worlds for old, was taking hold of the liberal imagination. Brooks was not to be blinded by the popular view of Wells to the more compelling truth that grave warnings, even hopelessness, lay at the storyteller's spiritual center.

Lately, after decades of neglect, a small coterie of critics both in England and the United States has been reappraising the earlier works of Wells, especially the scientific romances; and these men are finding that, at the core, these works are imaginative projections of Thomas Huxley's pessimism. These critics ignore the easy optimism of Wells's journalism for the clear grain of pessimism running through nearly all his artistic work. One of them, Anthony West, goes so far as to declare that Wells "had known the worst that there is for man to know about himself and his fate from the beginning, and he had faltered only in sharing his knowledge." [15]

If the starting-point of Wells's literary career is a series of scientific romances which invoke through myth and symbol their creator's fear that man could well be doomed by a hostile universe, the middle period shows Wells discarding the cosmos for the individual. Most of the novels that follow the golden trio of *Kipps, Mr. Polly,* and *Tono-Bungay* exhibit Wells wrestling unsuccessfully with the conflicts of his persona. Under a heavy film of doctrinaire musings are revealed such Wellsian alter-egos as the politician Remington in *The New Machiavelli* and the scientist Trafford in *Marriage,* men who come to grief through irrational compulsions within themselves.

In his search for a congenial persona, the influence of Huxley on Wells became much more than cerebral. Viewed through a dual lens as hero and as awesome abstraction, Huxley became the basis for the earliest shape of the Wells self-image: Herbert George Wells, Man of Science. Huxley loomed from lecture-platform vantage as the prototype for the first of Wells's fictional heroes, the scientist who would do battle with Jekyll-Hyde and Dr. Frankenstein. [16]

It is in the translating of the treacheries of evolution into scientific romance that one finds the authentic mood of H. G. Wells. One turns to the early tales where Huxley-Wells as knight-errant plays at war with alien forces in time and space. These visions, whose surface pyrotechnics conceal anti-utopian intimations, brought H. G. Wells to the attention of the literary world and may eventually prove his most lasting contribution to it.

CHAPTER 2

The Fall from Grace

I The Early Landscape

LESS than two decades have passed since the death, in his eightieth year, of H. G. Wells. To one not old enough to be of the generation nurtured on his books and yet old enough to remember "H. G. Wells" as a household name, it has been disheartening to watch the fall of his literary star. Most of this writer's contemporaries—those in their twenties when World War II broke out—usually remember Wells either as the author of that ballast to everyone's library, *The Outline of History,* or as somehow associated with that other, more glamorous, Welles—Orson—in the staging of a Martian invasion on a national radio network in 1938.

Wells's fall from grace began, of course, long before his pen was stilled by death. His literary life presented the spectacle of a writer making the complete cycle from artist to pamphleteer. His first success, *The Time Machine* (1895), had myth-making implications for an age just awakening to Darwin and Marx. But what made a giant of the creator of this and other fin-de-siècle scientific romances was narrative verve and story-telling magic. A half-dozen Realistic novels, written during a golden decade at the start of the present century, brought him comparison with Dickens in ability to create character freshly and engagingly.

The early fictional landscape of H. G. Wells is a canvas by Bruegel. One glimpses, along with the first sight of the spearhead ship of an invasion from Mars, a group of village urchins tossing stones at the cylinder that has fallen from the sky. One hears the bark of a cart-driver as he pulls up at Iping Village with the luggage of the Invisible Man. One follows Mr. Polly into a roomful of similarly dispossessed tradesmen after his "bit of arson" has destroyed the Fishbourne Hotel, but has also made a lion of him for rescuing his landlord's mother-in-law. One smells horse manure and beer, and hears, in V. S. Pritchett's description, the accent of the lower middle-class from which Wells sprung—"despairing, narrow-voweled yet truculent, with something of the cheapjack and Sunday League in it." [1]

This landscape of disorder is the creation of a man who, from firsthand, understood the private ordeals inherent in social struggle, and who extolled that struggle with a gusto second only to that of Dickens. Thus was the gaily trotting Wells, owner of the garrulous cockney squeak that so astounded Americans when they heard it for the first time on radio during the early months of World War II, enlisted for a limited time in the cause of comic literature. For a decade and a half, in his journey from South Kensington science student and tutor to grand statesman of British letters, he subordinated his message to the private dramas of his villagers.

However, following in the novel a trail blazed in the theater by Ibsen and Shaw, Wells soon forfeited any promise of joining the first rank of novelists. He found he could not be satisfied unless his characters stood for the multitudinous conflicts he saw in the world about him. After 1910 his characters began more and more to speak in Wellsian terms. They incited change and argued back and forth about every subject under the sun. As spokesmen for their creator, they reflected the searching discontent of the man whom Anatole France considered the leading intellectual force of the English-speaking world. [2]

The Bruegel landscape becomes a newsreel. There is a gradual blurring of the countryside until 1916; with *Mr. Britling Sees It Through,* a major best-seller in the United States, [3] the *mise en scène* is, in effect, a conference room. Of course, Wells maintains enough interest in Mr. Britling as a fallible human to temper the novel's heavy ideological content with a generous dosage of characterization. By 1916, however, characterization is only an engaging digression with Wells. *Mr. Britling,* essentially a document, albeit an invaluable one for students of World War I, sounded the notes for Wells's future novel-music: fewer and fewer Pollys and Kippses, more and more ideas and theories. This novelist was the H. G. Wells who for the final three decades of his career wrote tracts disguised as fiction, and did so in pursuit of an equilibrium, a world order, which the humanist in him knew was unattainable. [4] However, more truly, this was the disorderly H. G. Wells who, like the Mr. Lewisham of his first Realistic novel, destroyed his schema, his timetable, on the book's final page; the Wells who knew with the sure intuition of the artist that disequilibrium rules the human condition.

Thus Wells essayed the impossible: a leap over his shadow. For half his life the man he *was* conflicted with the man he thought he *ought* to be. The only value of his later idea-novels, of those symposiums in which the main character is always some alter ego of Wells, is to prove beyond doubt that, to the day of his death, H. G. Wells was never able to resolve the conflicting claims of what Jung calls the persona, man's most private and cherished conception of himself.[5]

II *Popularizer of Science*

If it was Wells's misfortune to live to see his once-cherished writings reduced to a parody of the novel-a-year automaton, he merits full credit for the estimable virtues of his defects. As an often inspired popularizer, he did more than any other man of letters to prepare the world for the age of science.[6] The clearing away of the darkness of the Victorian era, which claimed his father, his brothers, and almost himself as victims, proved to be his lifelong mission. Since the means to this end was a student's ticket from the Home Counties to South Kensington, it was no wonder that scientific knowledge and invention became for Wells the only keys to leaving Victorian opacity—any opacity—in the shadows behind him. Wells wrote his scientific romances between 1895 and 1904—strategic years when, as Horace Gregory states, "people of the Western Civilization held greatest hope for the promises of a new world opening up to them in progress of a 'scientific' twentieth century."[7]

When forays into interplanetary warfare and the future palled, Wells took up directly the problems of his day. Shaw always chided "our H.G." for being the most impatient of men, and it was this characteristic that betrayed Wells into placing less and less distance between Wells the artist and Wells the partisan. Nonetheless, his social novels, collectively, provide perhaps the most fully documented transcript of English lower middle-class life during the reigns of Edward VI and George V.[8]

Between the scientific romances of Wells's earliest period and the "idea" novels that occupied him after 1910, came *Kipps* (1905), *Tono-Bungay* (1909), and *The History of Mr. Polly* (1910). The trilogy is richly comic in a vein somewhere between Dickens and James Thurber. They deal with the only segment of society Wells knew from total immersion: the world of drapers and shopkeepers, cockney types who, like his father and brothers, lived out their lives in the rigidly deterministic world into which they were thrust.

By the time he wrote *Mr. Polly*, Wells had illustrated once again, according to George Orwell, that the creative writer has about fifteen years during which he is at the height of his powers.[9] Virtually all of his finest work was done between 1895 and 1910. His influence on the intelligentsia began to wane after World War I, but his standing as a household name was bolstered by the phenomenal popularity of *The Outline of History* (1920). H. G. Wells became during the first third of this century more than the writer of such-and-such a book: he took on the guise of a "term."[10] Awareness of Wells's impact prompted a once-close friend, even in a mood of bitter rancor, to acknowledge that those years could justly be called "The Age of H. G. Wells."[11] His passing as a serious influence also witnessed, as Gerald Heard has rightly observed, the end of Utopianism, "that specific mythos of the Modern Age, the Faith which took the place left by the gap when the Dantesque Divine Comedy closed with the close of the Middle Ages."[12] One is obliged here, however, to point to Wells's failure to take Hitler seriously in the 1930's and to his writing off Marx as indexes of his flagging perception.

Wells, more than any other writer, ushered in the century with an air of "anything is possible." For a time his blueprints for new worlds, his heralding of a time when man's intellect would liberate him from the bondage of hereditary misery and the inertia of inherited comfort, caught the imagination of countless thinking men. As a stimulant for thought and as a major bulldozer in clearing away the jungle caused in Britain by hundreds of years of muddle-headed political, theological and romantic-historical teaching, he ruled, with Shaw, supreme in his time.

Like Shaw, Wells grew more cautious as he went on. World War I loosed darkly irrational forces in men; and, though a careful reading of Wells's scientific romances and the best of his early

Realistic novels, notably *Tono-Bungay* and *The New Machiavelli*, showed his deeply pessimistic strain, the image persisted that Wells was firmly convinced, in his own phrase, that education would win in the race with catastrophe.[13] "Later," as Van Wyck Brooks, firmly Wellsian until he outgrew his discipleship, sadly related in his memoirs, "the teaching of H. G. Wells lent itself to the saturnine jeers of an age that had lost all belief in the will and in progress."[14] Ironically, at least in terms of Wells, it was the unleashing of the atomic bomb on Hiroshima that raised the problem of the mere survival of mankind to uppermost concern; a force was unharnessed which Wells in 1914 had forecast with uncanny accuracy in *The World Set Free*. Under the conditions imposed by the Atomic Age, all questions of the "good life"—the state of bliss to which Wells's men-like-gods could hopefully aspire—had to be deferred.

III *Catologues of Forebodings*

It has been easy for the newer wave of critics who have read their Eliot, Kafka, and Sartre to misread Wells. In the twenty years since his death, and also during the fallow years of his decline, H. G. Wells has been made the scapegoat for what Anthony West calls "the nineteenth-century progressive fallacy [and] blind faith in science."[15] Actually, the fruits of Wells's best period, garnished by storytelling virtuosity, are in the form of grave warnings to mankind.[16] It was mainly the doctrinaire journalism of a later Wells, a world-famous but sorely displaced person, which in West's words kept "promising mankind a birthday every week with gorgeous presents if scientists were only given their heads."[17]

Wells's major works form a catalogue of forebodings: the end of intellectual life in *The Time Machine;* the resort to something very like brainwashing in "The Country of the Blind"; moral collapse traceable to the consequences of the Darwinian revolution in *The Island of Dr. Moreau;* the catastrophe of uncontrolled experimentation in *The Invisible Man;* capitalistic charlatanry in *Tono-Bungay;* the development of intelligence at the expense of human sympathy in *The War of the Worlds;* the menace of war-prone earthlings to the lunar people in *The First Men in the Moon;* and the destructive consequences of irrational impulses in *The New Machiavelli*.

[28]

His old friend and co-conspirator Bertrand Russell is certainly correct when he constrains the reader to regard Wells as an important force toward sane and constructive thinking, "both as regards social systems and as regards personal relations." [18] If his detractors disagree and charge Wells with a fatal astigmatism for his apparent faith in the inevitable triumph of common sense, they should go back to his works of original inspiration: those cosmic voyages unsurpassed by any imaginative writer and those intimations of richer possibilities in human relationships passed on to a writer with whom few would link him, D. H. Lawrence.[19]

The long neglect accorded Wells is deserved only in terms of thirty years' sterile production at the end of his life. This hollow fecundity lapsed Wells's earlier claims and caused, as Mark Schorer believes, his escape "from literature into the annals of an era." [20] But H. G. Wells, myth-maker and poet, creator of the Time Traveller and the Invisible Man, clamors to be read, even as those literary progenitors of Walter Mitty—Mr. Polly and Artie Kipps—deserve a new audience.

CHAPTER 3

The Scientific Romances

LITERARY immortality is fickle at best, and the verdict of the ages is often ironic. It would be interesting to know what Jonathan Swift and Daniel Defoe, eighteenth-century literary kinsmen of Wells, would have answered had they been asked what they thought of their chances with the ages; if, more specifically, they had any inkling when they wrote *Gulliver's Travels* and *Robinson Crusoe* that the two books were destined to be read by every schoolchild. Answering honestly, Swift would probably have acknowledged that his book, originally published anonymously, was a scathing tract on courts, political factions, and statesmen that was written while his own disappointments still rankled. Defoe most certainly would have admitted *Crusoe* to be journalism, written as a feuilleton and about as mortal as its grandchild, the signed newspaper column.

Wells's best scientific romances have come down to us with the freshness of adventure stories. Their most insistent qualities are those of myth. Such romantic ideas as travel into past and future time, Martian invasion, invisibility, and lunar voyaging may not have originated with Wells; but a lifetime after he gave expression to them, he is still their principal spokesman. To an older generation of science-fiction readers, the photographs of Major Edward White taking his space hike in the summer of 1965 and the accelerating reports of Unidentified Flying Object sightings this year (1966) may have seemed, in some curious way, familiar. Looking at the pictures of the American astronaut astride the universe in a kind of cosmic sleep-walk recalls imagery from *The First Men in the Moon,* written by Wells in 1901. And who can say that the reports of U.F.O. sightings are not a response to the human urge for wonderment in an age of computers; an urge to return to anything-is-possible times like 1898, when Martians invaded London in *The War of the Worlds,* or, like 1938, when the Martians of another Welles—Orson—landed, via a national radio network, in Grover Mill, New Jersey?

As with the Swift and Defoe classics, stories like *The Time Machine, The Invisible Man, The Island of Dr. Moreau,* and *The War of the Worlds* may be read only as thrilling stories. Yet all the scientific romances have Swiftian overtones and can be viewed on several levels. In considering five of these works in some detail, it will be best to look simultaneously at all sides of the early Wells—the imaginative storyteller and mythmaker, the intellectual skeptic invoking pessimistically the fin-de-siècle promised land.

I The Time Machine (*1895*)

Today, with satellite balloons twinkling by with timetable exactitude and with men being sped into orbit in two ideological hemispheres, it may be difficult to imagine the impact of a work like *The Time Machine* in its period. With it, H. G. Wells made "the shape of things to come" a romantic phrase. But this first of Wells's scientific romances may be read, as youthful readers all over the world still affirm, entirely as a thrilling story of cosmic adventure in which the Time Traveller invents a machine of gleaming nickel and quartz that carries him along the Fourth Dimension, first to the world of 802701 A.D. with its degenerate descendants of man, and then on to the earth in its death agony.

The short novel opens at the home of a man identified only as "the Time Traveller." The host expounds on a theory of Time as the Fourth Dimension. He shows his small circle of friends first a working model, then the actual Time Machine. A week later the narrator goes again to the home of the Traveller, and this time the assembled group is told of his first and only flight into time. On the saddle of the machine he had flung himself far into futurity, stopping at the year 802701. He finds the Thames Valley a magnificent garden; London has disappeared save for gigantic but crumbling palaces of granite, marble, and aluminum. Mankind has differentiated into two races, the Eloi and the Morlocks. The Eloi are fragile, childlike people and, with the exception of Weena, a girl he saves from drowning, take little interest in him or in his machine. The machine is mysteriously stolen, and it is only then that he realizes the existence of the Morlocks, a bestial people who live in caverns and passages beneath the surface of the earth and who allow the Eloi to possess the earth on sufferance. They feed and clothe the Eloi from long habit, and prey upon them for their meat. After several adventures with the Morlocks, during one of which Weena is killed, the Traveller recovers the machine and travels once more into the future, until more than thirty millions of years have passed and the earth has at last come to rest with one face to the dull red sun, now so near as to obscure one tenth of the sky. Then he comes back, stopping his machine at eight o'clock on the evening of the day of his departure. Most of his guests incline to the belief that his tale is "a gaudy lie," and a few days later he sets out again with camera and knapsack to secure proof of the reality of his time-travelling. From the instant of his departure he is never seen again.

This plot summary, familiar even to the children of parents who no longer read Wells as avidly as their own parents did, does scant justice to what a leading science fiction writer, Arthur C. Clarke, recently called one of the two works of science fiction that are also literature.[1]

For a generation yet to hear of Albert Einstein, the opening pages of *The Time Machine* provided an introduction to the possibilities of the Fourth Dimension which in 1895 was not elsewhere available outside of scientific journals. The reader is initiated convincingly into the shaded-light-and-fireplace world of the Time Traveller and his friends ("The fire burned brightly, and the soft radiance of the incandescent lights . . . caught the bubbles that flashed and passed in our glasses"). The technique is one Wells's critics were to insist he borrowed from his ideological opposite number, Kipling; but, whatever the source of the device, it succeeded in providing a firm transport from ordinary contemporary life to an imaginative world beyond the ken of the late Victorian bourgeoisie.[2] By ushering his friends gathered about the shaded light into the world where a fourth dimension is possible, Wells shows himself to be essentially not, as Oscar Wilde had once said, "an English Jules Verne," [3] a forecaster of new inventions based on old models or, as with Poe, a searcher after "effects." Rather, using the currency of narrative fiction, he became the supreme communicator in his time of the possibilities of science.

[32]

Exciting as this narrative may be, *The Time Machine,* according to Mark R. Hillegas, "will also be read by the thoughtful at the much deeper level of its serious attack on human complacency." [4] Projected ahead into the world of the year 802701, the Time Traveller encounters a society that has split into two degenerate factions, with its intellectual life ended. Above ground live the Eloi, tiny creatures as gentle as butterflies, with the intellect of five-year-olds; below ground are the predatory, inhuman Morlocks, creatures who at night leave their dungeons to hunt down the Eloi for food.

Wells is quite explicit about what caused the collapse of man's utopian dream. Huxley, he says, was justified in his fears that mankind ultimately would be powerless to control the evolutionary process. For a time, perhaps for centuries, the millennium-promising balance between capital above ground and workers below was achieved. But it was destroyed because the Upper Worlders, the descendants of nineteenth-century capitalists, ignored Huxley's most salient warning: "If we may permit ourselves a larger hope of abatement of the essential evil of the world . . . I deem it an essential condition of the realization of that hope that we cast aside the notion that escape from pain and sorrow is the proper object of life." [5]

After the ancestors of the Eloi achieved security and freedom from danger, they lost the initiative that stems from struggle; their descendants evolved, therefore, to "mere feeble prettiness" and became the delicate Eloi. Only the knowledge of machinery prevented the Morlocks from enervating into vegetable-like creatures; but, when starvation ultimately became a world problem, Huxley's fears were realized with the reversion of the Morlocks to a state of cannibalism. The agency of destruction, Wells makes perfectly clear, was a materialist, technological society of the kind to which he, in a later phase, seemingly gave willing endorsement:

I grieved [muses the Time Traveller] at how brief the dream of human intellect had been. It had committed suicide. It had set itself steadfastly toward comfort and ease, a balanced society with security and permanency as its watchword. It had attained its hopes—to come to this at last. Once, life and property must have reached almost absolute safety. The rich had been assured of his wealth and comfort, the toiler assured of his life and work. No doubt in that perfect world there had been no unemployed problem, no social question left unsolved. And a great quiet had followed. (pp. 56–57)

The H. G. Wells of unforgettable stories like *The Time Machine* believed that men were as base and cruel as the Morlocks or as acquiescent as the Eloi. The world might easily become Dr. Moreau's island where, as will be shown in the next section, science produced destruction and death. In time, the Wells with a world-order obsession repudiated the authentic Wells of intuitive impulse, and the profound tug-of-war within him produced the dying curse against humanity in his last book, *Mind at the End of Its Tether* (1945).

Escaping the Morlocks by re-entering the time machine, the Traveller stops his conveyance for a look at the expiring world. Wells's picture of the world in lethargy is unforgettable. He has propelled his Traveller thirty million years ahead to a world in which man has disappeared. Although the huge sun obscures a tenth of the heavens, the air is bitter cold and snow is falling. Not even the gigantic crablike creatures, seen earlier in his journey, remain. The Traveller sees the last animated creature, a round thing the size of a football, trailing tentacles against the blood-red water.

In reading these passages, called by Nicholson "among the most significant (for the humanist) in the popular literature of the last sixty years," [6] one thinks of T. S. Eliot's Prufrock and his evocation of world's end desperation: "I should have been a pair of ragged claws scuttling/across the floors of silent seas." In horror at his vision of the full circle of evolution, the Traveller climbs weakly into the saddle of the machine, the hands spin backward upon the dials, and presently he is back in the comfortable "Now" of his London home.

V. S. Pritchett confidently asserts that *The Time Machine* "will take its place among the great stories of our language." He sees in it a harkening back to the early eighteenth century and to the highest traditions of English narrative literature.[7] Winston Churchill found the story "not unworthy to follow . . . in the train of *Gulliver's Travels*." [8] Pritchett, however, places Swift's imaginative range and style in a loftier position; he says they stem from a humanity "denied to Wells because he arrived at the beginning, the crude beginning, of a new enlargement, whereas Swift arrived toward the end of one." [9]

The truth of Pritchett's synthesis is underscored by the knowledge that the origins of the story are rooted firmly in Wells's years as a student at the Royal College of Science. In 1887, the year he completed his courses under Huxley and others, Wells began work on a fantastic novel called *The Chronic Argonauts*. Serialized in fragmentary form in the *Science Schools Journal* in April, May, and June of 1888, it was the first draft of *The Time Machine*, which did not appear for seven more years.[10] The *Time Machine* was an instant success; over six thousand copies were sold within a few weeks.[11] Although no overnight phenomenon, Wells clearly managed to capture the public ear at the very beginning of his literary career. No sooner had *The Time Machine* and his first collection of stories *The Stolen Bacillus* appeared, but he was deluged by inquiries from publishers. Writing to his mother, he said: "I've had letters too from four publishing firms asking for the offer of my next book. . . ." [12]

Although not widely reviewed, *The Time Machine* received favorable notices. One reviewer called it the most bizarre of fantasies since Stevenson's *Dr. Jekyll and Mr. Hyde* and lauded Wells for producing that rarity, a new thing under the sun.[13] The seventy years that have passed since its publication have seen no refutation of this tribute. Wells was the first writer to employ the idea of time as the fourth dimension in a story; and, so far as can be discovered, he invented the idea of travelling through time by means of a mechanical device.[14]

II   The Island of Dr. Moreau (*1896*)

It cannot be said, as with *The Time Machine,* that the second of Wells's major scientific romances falls outside the mainstream of English narrative fiction. As numerous critics have pointed out, *The Island of Dr. Moreau* owes immediate debts to Kipling's *Jungle Book,* to Mary Shelley's *Frankenstein,* and to the already-mentioned *Dr. Jekyll and Mr. Hyde.* Wells himself thought it a better book than *The Time Machine;* and, in terms of the shocking imagery of the work, his appraisal was accurate. *Moreau* is hard on the nerves, for the horror is more explicit than is usually possible in a clearly allegorical work.

Simply as a narrative, the story has scenes that are more suspenseful than anything found in its predecessor. A half-mad scientist, Moreau, has converted a Pacific island into a zoological laboratory. His fiendish work is discovered by another scientist, Edward Prendick, who has been shipwrecked and is picked up by a drunken assistant of Moreau. Prendick soon learns that there is nothing idyllic about Moreau's atoll retreat. The islanders are all grotesques. Despite semi-human appearance, they are unmistakably jungle creatures. They chant a Law which has been taught them by Moreau:

> Not to go on all-Fours; *that* is the Law.
> Are we not Men?
> Not to suck up Drink; *that* is the Law.
> Are we not Men?
> Not to eat Flesh nor Fish; *that* is the Law.
> Are we not Men?
> Not to claw Bark of Trees; *that* is the Law.
> Are we not Men?
> Not to chase other Men; *that* is the Law.
> Are we not Men?   (p. 105)

At first, Prendick, given a glimpse of Moreau at work on one of the creatures, assumes his aim is the transformation of men into animals and that he (Prendick) will be next. Only after he hears the latter part of the littany does he glean the whole truth:

> *His* is the House of Pain.
> *His* is the Hand that makes.
> *His* is the Hand that wounds.
> *His* is the Hand that heals.   (p. 105)

"A horrible fancy came into my head [reasons Prendick] that Moreau, after animalizing these men, had infected their dwarfed brains with a kind of deification of himself" (p. 105).

From this point, the story is the continuation in the life of that first Wellsian persona, the Time Traveller of the earlier story—

what Bergonzi calls the enlightened post-Darwinian scientist. The book, for the first time, projects a major confrontation which appears repeatedly in the scientific romances. Prendick seeks to overthrow Moreau's island laboratory and to release the beast-men from their bondage to pain and terror. He, like Wells, had studied under Huxley; and he held high the Huxleyan banner which proclaimed that the future could be shaped only by man's ethical control of the blind impulses of nature. Thus Prendick is made to stand for Huxley; Moreau, for Frankenstein.

The novel, illumining in fictional form Huxley's fears for the fate of homo sapiens, tells its story and delivers its myth-message in terms exemplified by a long line of island-allegory works, whose landmark is Shakespeare's *Tempest* and whose most recent addition is William Golding's *Lord of the Flies*. The genre's finest prose practitioners from Defoe to Golding have used the coral island as an elemental setting for parable and myth. Although neglecting to mention *Dr. Moreau*, Professor Carl Niemeyer has brilliantly traced the sources of *Lord of the Flies* (1954) to *Robinson Crusoe* (1719) and to R. M. Ballantyne's *The Coral Island* (1857).[15] Whereas the two earlier works extol the innate virtue of man, *Lord of the Flies*, like *The Island of Dr. Moreau*, traces the defects of society back to the defects of human nature.

Golding's book echoes the Ballantyne fable in its use of a group of castaway children who assume adult responsibility without adult supervision. Ballantyne endows his shipwrecked boys with pluck and resourcefulness so that they are able to subdue tropical islands as triumphantly as England imposes empire and religion on the lawless natives of the island. Golding, in an elaborate allegory of the end of civilization, leaves his boys to fend for themselves and shows that the beast, latent in all of them, may be subdued—and then only temporarily—by the organized institutions of civilization.

There are no children in *Dr. Moreau*, but the Wells book, written sixty years before *Lord of the Flies*, is an equally savage reaction against rampant optimism. Both authors develop, in the mythopoeic way that is their trademark, the idea that man is a savage, not intrinsically different from the Paleolithic brute. Humanity, as dramatized in the two novels, is but animal—rough-hewn to a reasonable shape and in perpetual conflict between instinct and injunction. "Morality in this view," writes Professor Leo J. Henkin, "is simply the padding of social and emotional habits by which society keeps the round Paleolithic savage in the square hole of the civilized state." [16] *The Island of Dr. Moreau* is a dramatization of this idea and is also a fictional elaboration on an article Wells wrote the same year, "Human Evolution, an Artificial Process." Wells assumes in *Moreau* that the gulf between animality and humanity is capable of being bridged by a surgeon's knife. Moreau's hybrids, walking on two feet and chanting their formula-like litany of the Law, slowly slip back into savagery. The beast folk, in Anthony West's words, "under Dr. Moreau's scar tissue . . . remain animals interested only in the satisfaction of their appetites." [17]

In Golding's novel, only one of the marooned boys, Simon, understands that there may indeed be a beast within each of the lads ("However Simon thought of the beast, there arose before his inward sight the picture of a human at once heroic and sick"). His intuition is verified in the mystic confrontation between Simon and the lord of the flies, a sow's head mounted on a stake. The sow has been killed savagely by the children. In worshipping the head, the youngsters satanically enthrone their own power of blackness. While the others hide from the truth behind masks, Simon hears the words of the "Lord": "Fancy thinking the Beast was something you could hunt and kill! You knew, didn't you? I'm part of you? Close, close, close! I'm the reason why it's no go? Why things are what they are?" Tragically, Simon is murdered by the boys because of their insane belief that he is the beast, the beast which he alone has exorcized through understanding.

In both books, the surviving representatives of civilization are rescued. In the later novel, Ralph leads a minority camp among the boys that is devoted to keeping the coral island at peace and to following the "rules." The British Navy arrives at the eleventh hour to save Ralph from the other camp, led by Jack Merridew, which is devoted to savagery and hunting. But until the rescue, Ralph and all he represents—that is, "parliament" or "human order"—was defeated, and Golding appears to be saying that adult society is lost in an even more hopeless way. In *The Island of Dr. Moreau*, Prendick's escape is even narrower. He is forced to become one of the beast people—the slayers of Moreau—until he can find a boat and set himself adrift. Returning to civilization, he, like Captain Gulliver after he has come back from the land of the Houyhnhnms, is horrified by contact with humans because their animal nature will never escape his memory. The island assumes its allegorical identity in his mind; it is the world where the brute in man is covered by the flimsiest of façades: "Then I look about me at my fellow men, and I go in fear. I see faces keen and bright, others dull or dangerous, others unsteady, insincere; none that have the calm authority of a reasonable soul. I feel as though the animal was surging up through them; that presently the degradation of the Islanders will be played over again on a larger scale." (p. 155).

For the two mythmakers, Wells and Golding, the beast in man will not inevitably backtrack into the jungle with the coming of rescue boats. Dr. Moreau's failure to make beast into man and the reversion of the boys into beasts are symbols of Thomas Huxley's fear that man may be the victim rather than the master of the cosmic process, both in nature and within himself. Wells endorsed Huxley's pessimistic declaration that "even the best of modern civilization appears to me to exhibit a condition of mankind which neither embodies any worthy ideal nor even possesses the merit of stability." [18]

The Island of Dr. Moreau was soundly thrashed by the critics for its sensationalism. *Athenaeum* devoted a long unfavorable review to the book without bothering to spell out its theme. A *Saturday Review* critic declared, "The horrors described by Mr. Wells in his latest book very pertinently raise the question how far it is legitimate to create feelings of disgust in a work of art." [19] Wells later described the book as "an exercise in youthful blasphemy. Now and then, though I rarely admit it [he said], the universe projects itself towards me in a hideous grimace . . . and I did my best to express my vision of the aimless torture in creation." [20]

Wells, in the heyday of his brilliant scientific romances, was the pessimistic pupil of Huxley. In his middle period, as will be seen, Wells turned away from the "hideous grimace" to a staunch faith in the cosmos, a faith which insisted, with the author of *The Origin of Species,* that "natural selection worked . . . for the good of each being (and) all corporeal and mental endowments will

tend to progress toward perfection." [21] Late in his life, as his utopian persuasion waned, Wells returned with a vengeance to the
intimations of *The Island of Dr. Moreau;* and they prompted him
to write that "our universe is not merely bankrupt; there remains
no dividend at all; it is going clean out of existence, leaving not a
wrack behind." [22]

III   The Invisible Man (*1897*)

None of the others can match the high spirit of Wells's third
scientific romance, *The Invisible Man,* but the influence of Huxley
is equally strong. The name of the scientist here has changed from
Prendick to Kemp, and the setting from the coral isle to Iping
Village in Surrey. Prendick battled a stranger, Dr. Moreau, but
Kemp confronts a former science college classmate, Griffin, who
has learned the secret of invisibility. The story's distinctive merits
stem from Wells's complete grasp of the Scottish meaning of
"weird": something which actually takes place. The story is an
adept balance between the unbelievable—the predicament of the
Invisible Man—and the ordinary—the routine life of Iping Inn.
The peculiar problem is Dashiell Hammett's "old chestnut" [23]—
making the reader feel that what cannot happen does happen
though it should not; and the writer's problem is compounded by
Wells's need to make the reader believe in invisibility without see-
ing it. To accomplish this feat, Wells presents the invisible Griffin
through the eyes of the villagers. His introduction is a montage of
increasingly bizarre effects: the hurrying figure swathed in band-
ages and wig, its mouth a gaping hole; its trouser legless, its sleeve
empty. It is a mesmerizing business; and, as Norman Nicholson
puts it epigrammatically, "we believe in all things visible and invisible." [24] *The Invisible Man,* in its early pages, is as picaresque as
the rural adventures of the bicycling Hoopdriver in *The Wheels
of Chance,* the first of the comic novels. The Coach and Horses
Inn of *The Invisible Man* derives from the same landscape as the
Fishbourne Hotel in the richly humorous *History of Mr. Polly.*
The ingenious explanation of how Griffin effected invisibility
demonstrates once again Wells's ability to project the possibilities
of science. Griffin, while working on the subject of optical density,
has hit upon a course of treatment whereby the refractive index of

human tissues may be equalized by that of the atmosphere, thus making the body invisible. The mood changes from Dickens to Kafka as Griffin is obliged by the consequences of his discovery to rob, kidnap, and eventually to murder.

Griffin's undoing, like Moreau's, stems from a megalomania that has convinced him that his discovery will endow him with unlimited power. Bernard Bergonzi is correct in stressing that, since Griffin's invisibility stands for Wells's apprehension of the possibilities of science, Griffin's fate must be seen as a rebuke for the pretensions of science and, perhaps, the end of the young Wells's own identification with a romanticized species of scientist-magician, one that is notably apparent in the characterization of the Time Traveller.

H. G. Wells, spinner of fables and maker of myths, is never so much in evidence as in the final scene, in which the Invisible Man, naked and in flight, is battered to death by the whirling spades of a desperate posse. Wells, the detached Huxleyan spokesman observing mankind rather than men, sees the dead Griffin physiologically—molecularly—and, at last, for just an instant, as human: "It [the transformation to visibility] was like the slow spreading of a poison. First came the little white nerves, a hazy grey sketch of a limb, then the glassy bones and intricate arteries, then the flesh and skin. . . . Presently . . . his crushed chest . . . the dim outline of his drawn and battered features [and finally] there lay, naked and pitiful on the ground, the bruised and broken body of a young man about thirty. . . ." (261).

This passage, one of the most memorable in all of Wells's books, is comparable to the glimpse of the dying world in *The Time Machine*. No writer of his day put so much power into an essentially detached viewpoint.[25] In his first three scientific romances Wells sees humans as stripped of their distinctly human qualities, just as Griffin is stripped of clothing to maintain transparency. Once again, as in *The Island of Dr. Moreau,* Wells is saying that not even the development of the secret of invisibility is in itself a guarantee of progress. Griffin has studied natural science and has become as pitiless as the elements. The cosmic process, declares Wells, in an echo of Huxley, is at odds with the ethical process. *The Invisible Man,* then, is a warning of what could happen if science, in the persons of the Griffins and Moreaus, is not controlled. The instruments of saving the world are the enlightened, humanity-based Kemps and Prendicks.

IV   The War of the Worlds (1898)

The *War of the Worlds* is the archetype of all B-Grade films which present giant creatures from another world who invade the earth armed with death-ray guns. The imagery of the novel is so vivid that it is no wonder film scenarists have always thought of outer-space invasions in Wellsian terms. Moreover, one grasps from this novel the essential technique of all of Wells's scientific romances, *Dr. Moreau* excepted: the pinning of strange events to an everyday locale. The attraction of *The Invisible Man* lay in placing the astounding dilemma of Griffin within the slow village life of Iping. In *The War of the Worlds,* the narrator sees the effects of the Martian invasion on a village in Woking, a place familiar to Wells because he once retreated there to convalesce from illness. Wells wrote in his autobiography of bicycling about the district and "marking down suitable places and people for destruction by my Martians." However, unless one counts Wells's characteristic chiding of the clergy in the sketch of a curate whose corner on salvation barely tides him over the invasion period, there is no evidence that Wells was writing autobiographically or even thought of his Woking villagers as individuals.

Combined with a faultless adherence to down-to-earth physical details is a sense of time; the chronology of invasion is attributable about equally to a boy's imaginative grasp of war games and to a man's foreboding vision of terrestrial resistance turned to panic:

About three o'clock there began the thud of a gun at measured intervals from Chertsey to Addlestone. I learnt that the smouldering pine-wood into which the second cylinder had fallen was being shelled in the hope of destroying that object before it opened. It was only about five, however, that a field gun reached Chobham for use against the first body of Martians.

About six in the evening, as I sat at tea with my wife in the summerhouse talking vigorously about the battle that was lowering upon us, I heard a muffled detonation from the common, and immediately after a gust of firing. Close on the heels of that came a violent rattling crash, quite close to us, that shook the ground; and, starting out upon the lawn, I saw the tops of the trees about the Oriental College burst into smoky red flame, and the tower of the little church beside it slide down the ruin. The pinnacle of the mosque had vanished, and the roof-line of the college itself looked as if a hundred-ton gun had been at work upon it. One of our chimneys cracked as if a shot had hit it, flew, and a piece of it came clattering down the tiles and made a heap of broken red fragments upon the flowerbed by my study window.

I and my wife stood amazed. Then I realized that the crest of May-berry Hill must be within range of the Martians' Heat-Ray now that the college was cleared out of the way. (pp. 288–89)

This extraordinary grasp of moment-to-moment detail made the novel easy prey for Orson Welles when in 1938 he converted it into the script which panicked a national radio audience. Welles changed the setting from a British district to Grover Mill, New Jersey. That he drew from Wells the essential imagery of the inva-sion can be seen by a comparison of the novel's description of the Martian emerging from the space-cylinder with that of the radio script. In *The War of the Worlds,* Wells writes:

A big greyish rounded bulk, the size, perhaps, of a bear, was rising slowly and painfully out of the cylinder. As it bulged up and caught the light, it glistened like wet leather.

Two large dark-coloured eyes were regarding me steadfastly. The mass that framed them, the head of the thing, it was rounded, and had, one might say, a face. There was a mouth under the eyes, the lipless brim of which quivered and panted, and dropped saliva. The whole creature heaved and pulsated convulsively. A lank tentacular append-age gripped the edge of the cylinder, another swayed in the air. (pp. 275–76)

In the scenario, the announcer gasps: "Good heavens, some-thing's wriggling out of the shadow like a grey snake. Now it's another one, and another. They look like tentacles to me. There, I can see the thing's body. It's large as a bear and it glistens like wet leather. . . . The mouth is V-shaped with saliva dripping from its rimless lips that seem to quiver and pulsate. . . ." [26]

Wells, apostle of the possible, registers himself in *The War of the Worlds* as the arch-enemy of the smug heralders of a new-century utopia in which the Union Jack would always prevail. "With infinite complacency," he writes in the opening paragraph of this novel about the routing of civilization, "men went to and fro over the globe about their little affairs, serene in their assurance of their empire over matter." Even as they luxuriate in a mental inertia of "all's well," keener intelligences from Mars covet the earth and lay plans to conquer it.

The same cautionary message, told in fable, is sounded in the previous romances: Man has no right to take control of the cosmic process for granted. Wells warns the reader to look at what happened to Mars—"not only more distant from life's beginning but nearer its end." The conditions on Mars became increasingly uncongenial to higher life, Wells speculated, citing dropping temperature, thinning atmosphere, water drying up. Eventually, the planet was forced to search space for some buffer to cosmic annihilation. Once again Wells reinforces his convictions by presenting a picture of the expiring planet of war as a preview of earth's fate: an earth moving in Huxleyan inexorability along the declining parabola of evolution.

Wells, in effect, gives the reader a step-by-step report on how a breakup of metropolitan society would come about. Whereas *The Time Machine* and the yet-to-come *First Men in the Moon* are conceived poetically—that is, the myths of time travel and of moon visitation are rendered in such a way as to suspend the demands of verisimilitude—in *The War of the Worlds* the mythpoeic mood is exchanged for the methods of documentary realism. The Martian invasion is treated as an event of contemporary history.

It is not necessary to review the invasion in detail. Suffice it to say that the Martians are octopus-like creatures who are as far above mankind in intellect and command of machinery as humans are above animals. The Martians stride over the earth in machines of impregnable armor and devastate town and country with searchlights projecting rays more destructive than those of radium. They feed on human blood, and they force humanity, if it is not to perish or become as docile as the Eloi, to seek subterranean refuge. In the robot-like calculations of the Martians, Wells again underscores Huxley: evolution may produce creatures with superior brains, but it will not inevitably lead to a millennium.

In one of Wells's best passages of dramatic sociological speculation, a courageous artilleryman speaks of what life will be like for

the survivors: "The tame ones [of us] will go like all tame beasts.
. . . The risk is that we who keep well will go savage—degenerate into a sort of big, savage rat. . . . You see, how I mean to live
is underground. I've been thinking about the drains. . . . Then
there's cellars, vaults, stores, from which bolting passages may be
made to the drains. And the railway tunnels and subways. Eh?
You begin to see? And we form a band—able-bodied, clean-
minded men. We're not going to pick any rubbish that drifts in.
Weaklings go out again" (pp. 371–72). The artilleryman's formula
is suggestive of the fallout fears of a more modern day which
Wells did not quite live to see. In *The War of the Worlds,* the
worldlings are relieved of the necessity of putting survival conditions to the test by the intervention of an unexpected ally, the
most minute of rescuers: the microbe. The invaders from Mars,
lacking immunity to terrestrial diseases, are annihilated by one of
them.

The possibility of life on Mars was part of the folklore in Britain
at the end of the nineteenth century. The first volume of Camille
Flammarion's *La Planète Mars* had appeared in 1892, thus making, as Bernard Bergonzi suggests, "a convenient and plausible
superhuman adversary for mankind." [27] Passages in Chapter I of
Wells's novel are probably imitations of Flammarion; they describe the physical conditions of Mars and are strikingly similar to
descriptions in Flammarion's books. Wells's theories of the super-
human qualities of the Martians were also in line with those of the
American astronomer Percival Lowell, who in 1896 advanced the
idea that the canals on Mars were the work of intelligent beings.[28]

But H. G. Wells's "scientific" knowledge of Mars, impressive as
it was, has in the years since the book's publication become secondary to the message that underlies the romance—a message few
of Wells's early readers understood. The novel continued his practice of bludgeoning the complacent bourgeois. He who had forced
his mean little undernourished and illness-ridden body out of
dingy shops was at century's end, by dint of the scientific romances, forcing himself on literary society.[29]

Who can say how many of Wells's dread forebodings in these
four novels had their origin in Huxley's laboratory and how many
in severe social maladjustment? The H. G. Wells of 1897, barely
thirty but soon to be famous, was encountering difficulties in gain-

ing acceptance in the cultivated world with its necessary insincerities and demand for credentials. It may be that the early Wells might have welcomed some such social upheaval concomitant upon invasion or similar catastrophe. As he wrote to his close friend George Gissing that very year, he might see in such an event, "a return to the essential, to honorable struggle as the epic factor in life. . . ." [30]

At any rate, the assertions of the coarse artilleryman, though somewhat discredited later in the novel, mark perhaps a beginning toward a new, sociological Wells—one who, within less than a decade, would project in a landmark utopian book, *A Modern Utopia,* a thoroughgoing blueprint for world revolution in the hands of an intellectual and physical élite, the Samurai. If, as St. John Ervine insists, sociology ruined H. G. Wells, the beginnings of that forty-year penchant may be gleaned even in a masterful scientific romance like *The War of the Worlds.*

V The First Men in the Moon (*1901*)

The First Men in the Moon has the same deceptive simplicity as *The Time Machine.* As the story of an imaginary journey into space, it represents, according to Mark Hillegas, "the highest point in the development of the cosmic voyage in the nineteenth century." [31] On perhaps its most profound level, the novel, and especially a long Gulliverian colloquy between the moon voyager and the Grand Lunar, is rich in satire. Although nearly always paired with Jules Verne's *From the Earth to the Moon,* the story draws more fundamentally from Swift; it shares with *Gulliver's Travels* a portrayal by parable of life on earth, or, in the case of Swift's disciple, of life within the rigidly class-divided structure of English society. Finally, the story stands at the apex of that handful of works which reveal what Nicholson calls Wells's "poetic gift." Nowhere in popular literature can one find so moving a description as that of the landing on the moon at the dawn of a lunar day—T. S. Eliot termed it "quite unforgettable" [32]—or so vivid a picture as that of the gigantic ant-hill of the moon's interior, with its blue-lit passageways and tunnels lying above the great swirling, luminescent central sea that laps around the moon's core.

Cosmic journeys were literary staples as early as the seventeenth century. The most famous of eighteenth-century voyagers

—Crusoe and Gulliver—chose water as their element. Jules Verne preceded Wells with his *From the Earth to the Moon* (1865), a book to which Wells acknowledged a greater debt than to any other nineteenth-century story of a cosmic voyage. But, as Hillegas points out, "it is difficult to pin down the numerous similarities and determine which are the result of direct borrowing by Wells and which are due to the feeling of a common tradition by the two authors." [33] Indeed, the differences are more to the point. Arnold Bennett was the first major writer to demur from the view that Wells was an English Verne. Bennett pointed to Verne's preoccupation with machinery over men; his stockpiling of unimportant scientific facts at the expense of story movement; the abortive nature of the voyage which relieved him of any necessity for those lunar descriptions which so distinguish the Wells book; the absence of a philosophical base. [34]

Verne immersed himself in mechanics. His method was to place his three explorers in a padded projectile and to shoot them from an enormous gun, the barrel of which was a well, sunk nine hundred feet in the ground and charged with four hundred thousand pounds of gun-cotton. Verne amassed, in the interest of scientific fidelity, material better suited to the lecture room: "The Armstrong cannon employs only 75 pounds of powder for a projectile of eight hundred pounds, and the Rodman Columbiad uses only one hundred sixty pounds of powder to send its half-ton shot a distance of six miles." The Frenchman went to great lengths to work out the mathematics of setting off his projectile. He, in effect, left to a better writer the lunar landscape by having his projectile deflected off course and finally reversed back to earth.

Wells, that better writer, took up where Verne left off. Verne was interviewed in 1903 and asked about Wells's moon novel. He scoffed at Wells for "inventing" and wanted to be shown gravity-resisting Cavorite. [35] The Englishman, on the other hand, was always fair to Verne: ". . . there is no literary resemblance whatever between the anticipatory inventions of the great Frenchman and my fantasies. . . ." [36]

Verne wished only to make his fictional product scientifically merchandisable. He, with Poe's balloonist Hans Pfaal, [37] drowned the lunar flight in a tide of documentation. Wells threw such caution to the winds. Never in his scientific romances did he worry

about technicalities. Without a machine equipped for the purpose, there would have been no time travel; but Wells gives little
description of the time-girdling conveyance. He brings to *First
Men* the invention of "Cavorite," a gravity-resisting substance
which enables his moon-voyagers, Bedford and Cavor, to travel to
the moon; and he permits Bedford eventually to return. Cavorite
is moored tenuously to the laws of physics. The writer Bedford,
the narrator, says from the outset that he took no notes while
Cavor explained his theories.

As was his custom, Wells domesticates his setting, keeping it
firmly Kentish: "It [Lympne] is in the clay part of Kent, and my
bungalow stood on the edge of an old sea cliff and stared across
the flats of Romney marsh at the sea" (p. 392). And Cavor is neither Frankenstein nor Moreau, but compounded of features
drawn by Boz: "He was a short, round-bodied, thin-legged little
man, with a jerky quality in his motions; he had seen fit to clothe
his extraordinary mind in a cricket cap, an overcoat, and cycling
knickerbockers and stockings. . . . He gesticulated with his
hands and arms and jerked his head about and buzzed. He
buzzed like something electric. You never heard such buzzing.
And ever and again he cleared his throat with a most extraordinary noise" (p. 393). Cavor foreshadows Artie Kipps and Mr.
Polly. The man comes alive as Verne's cosmic voyagers never do.

No less realistic are the strokes Wells uses to disclose that there
is life on the moon. His deft touches never leave the reader without solid associations:

I have said that amidst the stick-line litter were these rounded bodies,
these little oval bodies that might have passed as very small pebbles.
And now first one and then another had stirred, had rolled over and
cracked, and down the crack of each of them showed a minute line of
yellowish green, thrusting outward to meet the hot encouragement of
the newly risen sun. . . .

Every moment more of these seed coats ruptured, and even as they
did so the swelling pioneers overflowed their rent-distended seed-cases,
and passed into the second stage of growth. With a steady assurance,
a swift deliberation, these amazing seeds thrust a rootlet downward to
the earth and a queer little bundle-like bud into the air. In a little
while the whole slope was dotted with minute plantlets standing at
attention in the blaze of the sun. . . .

The movement was slower than any animal's, swifter than any plant I have ever seen before. How can I suggest it to you—the way that growth went on? The leaf tips grew so that they moved onward even while we looked at them. The brown seed-case shrivelled and was absorbed with an equal rapidity. Have you ever on a cold day taken a thermometer into your warm hand and watched the little thread of mercury creep up the tube? These moon plants grew like that. (p. 425)

Passages like this can only derive from the marriage of scientist and literary artist. Wells clearly drew on what must have been his feelings the first time he looked into a microscope at South Kensington. He used myriad images remembered from the study of botany, making a kind of collage full of suggestive effects. Wells never quite lost this gift for rendering evolution—the growth of species, human, animal or plant—poetically. It shimmers through the early pages of *The Outline of History* in those sections devoted to prehistoric man.

The action of the story properly starts when the voyagers find that there is not only plant but human life on the moon. For Wells's purposes, super-creatures like the Martians will not do. This time the Selenites, far from towering over the earthlings like the tentacled invaders of *The War of the Worlds*, are ant-like. Like Swift's Lilliputians, whose descendants they assuredly are, they capture the Gullivers from earth. Cavor and companion are taken inside the moon; after a grim struggle that suggests the Time Traveller's battle with the Morlocks, they escape. The two separate, and Cavor is again made prisoner. Bedford finds the sphere and returns to earth. The rest of the story is told by virtue of an invention that necessarily eluded Verne: wireless. Cavor's messages are devoted to a description of the moon-creatures—the insect breed which by vocational specialization has developed into a species with hundreds of varieties, each adapted for a single job.

Here Wells delves further into an idea that fascinated him as early as *The Time Machine* and *The War of the Worlds*, an idea which finds expression in all the utopian novels which he wrote until almost the end of his life. Wells believed that the specialization brought on by scientific advances would cause structural modifications of the individual. In *First Men*, for instance, the machine-minders have enormously developed hands; and memory-men, there being no books or writing on the moon, have enormous craniums and shrunken torsos. In a much later novel of Wells's more sanguine phase—*Men Like Gods* (1923)—the utopians wear no clothes, their lives having progressed to a state of unalloyed bliss.

No such optimism tempered the mood of the man who closed out his major scientific romances with *The First Men in the Moon*. The society of the Selenites reflects Huxley's cosmic pessimism at its blackest by exposing planned civilization at its worst. The adaptation and control of the organism produces efficiency in the moon-people and resolves instability caused by the struggle for existence, but human considerations are muted. In fact, it is impossible not to read into *The First Men in the Moon* a Wellsian commentary on Marxist theory. Georges Connes in *Étude sur la Pensée de Wells* (1926) draws a reverse analogy between revolution as promised by Marx and the evolvement of Wells's lunar society to a state of greater control by the few and stricter obedience by the many.[38] Revolution, in fact, is rendered impossible by the acquiescence of the Selenites to super-efficient specialization. The satire contained in Cavor's wire, telling how young Selenites are compressed in jars with only their elongated hands free to be trained for machine-minding, hints at Wells's suspicion that a society that makes its members into automatons is the worst kind of slave system. Efficiency has replaced morality.

The kind of technological utopia with which the popular image of Wells is associated was anathema to him in the five major scientific romances. Not efficiency but "freedom of mind"—the peace of Plato's idealism—is at the center of Wells's utopia. At the end of the book, Cavor's messages end. It is clear he has been slain by his captors. Unwisely, he had allowed the Selenites to glimpse earth's imperialistic tendencies, its penchant for war. In the fear that Cavor might "contaminate" the Selenites, the Grand Lunar found no alternative to killing him. Cavor's fatally revealing interview with the Grand Lunar appears to have been modeled after Gulliver's audience with the king of Brobdingnag.[39] Lacking Swift's end-of-era misanthropism, Wells, writing at the start of a technological age, was content to warn readers of the dangers of unchecked scientific materialism.

CHAPTER 4

Literary Edison: The Short Stories

H. E. BATES praises Wells as "a great Kidder . . . a man who succeeded in telling more tall stories than any writer of his generation yet, by a genius for binding the commonplace to the most astronomical exploration of fancy, succeeded in getting them believed." [1] In the previous chapter it was seen how the best of the scientific romances persuade by making the cannot-happen thing into the does-happen-but-shouldn't; the short stories use the same device. An inexperienced ghost forgets his formula; a Mittyesque Cockney eats a berry and turns into a termagant; a man undergoing an operation has, like Conrad Aiken's Mr. Arcularis, a dream in which he dies, and the earth bearing his deserted body spins away while his mind remains to span a thousand years in seconds;[2] a diving-bell descends into the deep, and its occupant finds a city of reptiles who worship him.

The stories may well be, as Frank Swinnerton has said, the "most characteristic" of Wells's works.[3] They—some seventy of them were published—are products of the storyteller's art, written at a time when Wells was struggling to become launched as a writer, and long before the teacher-propagandist silenced the teller of tales.

Wells, who seems always to have known a marketable literary commodity when he saw it, started writing short stories at a propitious time. In the 1890's, the golden age of the English short story had begun. Kipling's stories of Anglo-Indian life were opening a new and exotic dimension to readers in several continents, Poe and his theory of the well-made story had become a pattern for imitation, and a flourishing de Maupassant community had come into existence on the English side of the Channel. Wells's range is narrower than Kipling's, only rarely does Wells achieve effects anywhere near Poe's, and Wells is incapable of the irony underlying the deceptively simple studies of de Maupassant. But from these three masters H. G. Wells discovered the technique of the short story. "I was doing my best to write as the other writers wrote," he acknowledges in his autobiography; "and it was long before I realized that my exceptional origins and training gave me an almost unavoidable freshness of approach." [4]

Wells came to realize that his knowledge of science gave him a vantage point for writing a kind of story which was out of the reach of Kipling, Poe, and de Maupassant. He soon occupied himself writing tales of the strange, which frequently described and usually extended some innovation of science or technology. In a progressive age, his visioning in 1903 of tank warfare ("The Land Ironclads") and of aerial flight as early as 1897 ("The Argonauts of the Air") combined the topical with the novel in affairs. Only two months after the flying-machine story had been published, a flight similar to the one detailed in the story, also climaxed by an accident, took place over Berlin. Camille Flammarion was one of the first to describe modern types of aircraft in fiction, but Wells pioneered in making a mishap in a flying machine the object of treatment in a story.[5]

Early readers of Wells's tales, then, had the impression that they were being let in on something that had just happened, was happening, or was about to happen. However, the best stories transcend the merely topical. These, like the scientific romances, have the power to imbue the reader with a sense of personal freedom. Spirits soar; inhibitions fade. And the mood is sustained as it is only rarely in Wells's Realistic novels. That mood is nearly always the same—one of exhilaration, of anything-is-possible, even of awe. The tales all have the same message: how much worldlings could do—how much might come to pass—if they just let their fancy take off a bit from ground-level.[6]

The impetus to write these stories was first provided by Lewis Hind, then (1894) the editor of *Pall Mall Gazette,* who invited the twenty-eight-year-old Wells to contribute a series of "single-sitting" stories. Fifteen were published as a book in the same year (1895) that *The Time Machine* came out. Ingvald Raknem, after exhaustive research into the early criticism which heralded Wells, observes how much in fashion the twenty-nine-year-old author was: his *Stolen Bacillus and Other Incidents* was one of fifteen collections of stories reviewed in *The Athenaeum* of December 21, 1895.[7]

I   *The Fantasies*

"The Stolen Bacillus," the title story of Wells's maiden collection, not only is representative but is also the first of his "single-sitting" stories. It contains seedlings of *The Invisible Man, The War of the Worlds,* and *The History of Mr. Polly.* A bacteriologist tells a romantically inclined anarchist that he has imprisoned cholera bacillus in a test-tube—enough, if introduced into the drinking supply, to bring pestilence to London. The anarchist, intent on destruction, steals the bottled cholera. The scientist pursues him by horse-cab and a maid-servant, anxious that the scientist not catch his death, brings up the rear carrying his coat. The scene flares into comic disarray, not unlike Mr. Polly's burning of the Fishbourne Hotel, with the three-way race described by a group of Cockneys. In his haste, the anarchist cracks the tube and, bent on martyrdom, drinks the potion. The bacteriologist confesses to his maid that he had only tried to astonish his visitor; that, far from being cholera bacillus, it was the bacterium bringing out blue patches in monkeys.

The story bears the early hints of Wells's penchant for superimposing exotic material from the laboratory on the prosaic lives of the lower-middle-class Wells knew so well. "The Stolen Bacillus" also reveals a strain of jolly humor amidst the most serious of possibilities, one which Wells was to retain in his writings and in his life almost to the end. The anarchist and the scientist appear ludicrous to the spectators, the dire aspects of the chase notwithstanding. Griffin in *The Invisible Man,* with all his transparency, rampaged more picaresquely than formidably until he went berserk and had to be destroyed.

A famous story, "The Man Who Could Work Miracles" (1898), is archetypal of a vast literature about unprepossessing souls unexpectedly endowed with the power to upset their worlds. The clerk Fotheringay was an early model for Thorne Smith's Topper. Topper cavorted invisibly, but Fotheringay had real room for enterprise: his supreme windfall lay in conjuring up miracles. But, as with so many who lack the proper combination of élan and restraint for the proper use of divine powers, Fotheringay let his reach exceed his grasp. Requesting that the earth stop rotating, he precipitated a scene of comic confusion as every object about him fell off into space.

II *The Parables*

If Wells in those early stories gave dramatic and sometimes bizarre expression to his feelings about the infinite plasticity of things, he was also capable, within the confines of the short story form, of spinning parables to illustrate his distrust of perfected civilization. In a story like "The Lord of the Dynamos," the symbolic implications become more emphatic than in the "trick" fantasies. The first paragraph dramatizes one of Wells's polemical positions—hatred of Empire. The reader is introduced to the uncivilized-civilized white man, the characteristically wooden product of technological society, and to his "burden" who will rise against oppression and destroy:

> The chief attendant of the three dynamos that buzzed and rattled at Camberwell and kept the electric railway going, came out of Yorkshire, and his name was James Holroyd. He was a practical electrician but fond of whisky, a heavy red-haired brute with irregular teeth. He doubted the existence of the Deity but accepted Carnot's cycle, and he had read Shakespeare and found him weak in chemistry. His helper came out of the mysterious East, and his name was Azuma-zi. But Holroyd called him Pooh-bah. Holroyd liked a nigger because he would stand kicking—a habit with Holroyd—and did not pry into the machinery and try to learn the ways of it. Certain odd possibilities of the negro mind brought into abrupt contact with the crown of our civilization Holroyd never fully realized, though just at the end he got some inkling of them. (p. 277)[8]

Holroyd is pictured as a brute of the sort who, seventy-five years before the story saw print, had imposed an uncongenial order on the aboriginal population of Tasmania and had concluded by forcing its extinction. Wells acknowledged that conversations with his brother Frank about Tasmania had led to *The War of the Worlds*. At about the same time, his mentor Huxley was citing the extinction of the natives of that country as a tragedy of evolution.[9]

Holroyd and Azuma-zi, white man and "white man's burden,"

are opposed on all points: the positivism of the one contrasts with the superstitious nature of the other. Like Yank in O'Neill's *Hairy Ape*, Azuma-zi learns to worship the dynamo but for all the wrong reasons:[10] "Holroyd delivered a theological lecture on the test of his big machine soon after Azuma-zi came. He had to shout to be heard in the din. 'Look at that,' said Holroyd; 'where's your 'eathen idol to match 'im?' And Azuma-zi looked. For a moment Holroyd was inaudible, and then Azuma-zi heard: 'Kill a hundred men. Twelve per cent on the ordinary shares,' said Holroyd, 'and that's something like a Gord!' " (p. 279). Wells fastens the electrician's religious intimations to the dynamo: it is a god to him because of its "kill-a-hundred-men" power and of its importance to the capitalist enterprise Wells would soon deride at length, if symbolically, in *The Time Machine*.

The climax of "The Lord of the Dynamos" is approached with a kind of dread inevitability rarely seen in Wells's longer fiction, except for *The Island of Dr. Moreau* and *The Invisible Man*. No polemic holds up the narrative; one feels the tightening of suspense. The native, under Holroyd's sneering tutorship, becomes a worshipper of the dynamo; and, by tribal custom, he must ritualize it. Azuma-zi one night grasps the lever and sends the armature in reverse. There is a struggle, and Holroyd is electrocuted. His death is taken to have been accidental, and a substitute arrives. For Azuma-zi, the newcomer is to be a second sacrifice. This time the Asiatic is foiled; to avoid capture, he kills himself by grasping the naked terminals of the dynamo. The conclusion is fittingly phrased in myth of undeniable power: "So ended prematurely the worship of the Dynamo Deity, perhaps the most short-lived of all religions. Yet withal it could at least boast a Martyrdom and a Human Sacrifice" (p. 286).

Wells's "Dynamo Deity" metaphor is suggestive of Henry Adams, who in *The Education of Henry Adams* refers to the Virgin Mary as the "animated dynamo." Adams, like the H. G. Wells whom E. M. Forster parodied in "The Machine Stops," conceived of man as a unit of energy capable of being attracted by powerful forces like the Virgin or the dynamo. It may even be that Wells, in this story of a primitive who tried to make a god of a dynamo, gave dramatic dimension to Adams's idea that "the movement of . . . forces controls the progress of [man's] mind, since he can know nothing but the motions which impinge on his senses, whose sum makes education." [11]

However, in a more seminal way, "The Lord of the Dynamos" is almost pure Kipling, and one feels a wave of sympathy for the misled Azuma-zi. Certainly, the story broadly conceives the meeting of the twain, East and West—the aboriginal Tasmanians and the British colonials. The work, writes Bernard Bergonzi in his brilliant book on Wells the mythmaker, recalls the early Joseph Conrad and *Heart of Darkness,* a novel not yet published when Wells wrote "Lord of the Dynamos" in 1894. Whether more Conradian or Kiplingesque is less important than that the story, like others among the handful by Wells that are consistently anthologized, can be read simply as a good yarn as well as for profounder implications beneath the parable.

In another of his earliest stories, "The Remarkable Case of Davidson's Eyes" (1895), Wells turns for the first time to the theme of what Bergonzi calls "the rootlessness and mental and emotional fragmentation of the modern intellectual." [12] More simply, Wells was preoccupied from the beginning of his career with the conflicting compulsions of art, which he saw as alienating the practitioner from the mainstream of life, and with the teaching of ideas, which increasingly he came to see as his proper business. The publication in 1886 of *Dr. Jekyll and Mr. Hyde,* Stevenson's vivid reiteration of Poe's "William Wilson," dramatized an emergent end-of-century myth: the discovery of the unconscious mind. In his later idea novels, Wells directly acknowledged a debt to Carl Jung and his conception of the struggle in men's minds between Consciousness and the Shadow, Jung's feeling of living simultaneously in two different ages and of being two different persons. [13]

In "The Remarkable Case," an undistinguished young scientist named Sidney Davidson suffers a dislocation of his vision while conducting an experiment. While he continues to be bodily present in London, he lives *visually* on an uninhabited isle somewhere on the other side of the earth. Wells's fancy in a story of this kind is inventive beyond compare. When Davidson is taken downhill in London, his vision similarly descends on the island, so that at certain points he sees and describes a strange maritime world of luminous fishes; but he can still hear people passing in the London street and a newsboy selling papers. Normal vision returns, and the extra-sensory world disappears. Years later a photograph proves to Davidson that the island did indeed exist, and the testimony of a ship's officer anchored offshore verifies the duality of Davidson's former life.

"The Story of the Late Mr. Elvesham," in which a young medical student named Eden enters into a kind of Faustian pact with an elderly stranger named Elvesham and enters the old man's body without losing his own mental identity, can also be taken as a play on the theme of spiritual schizophrenia.

By the time Wells stopped writing stories, the theme of self-alienation had flowered into a giant contempt for *ars pro arte*. Wells's last story, "The Pearl of Love" (1925), rejected that year by the editors of *The Saturday Evening Post* but subsequently published in England, dramatized the folly of projecting esthetic means for spiritual ends.[14] Twenty years before "The Pearl," however, Wells had practically stopped writing short stories. Two of his latter ones, among his best known, provide a poetic rendering of Wells's own personal obsessions as man and artist.

"The Beautiful Suit," first published in *Collier's* (April 1909) under the title "A Moonlight Fable," superficially follows the manner of a fairy tale by Oscar Wilde. A boy is presented by his mother with a shining suit but is constrained from wearing it, except on special occasions, by the poor woman's innate caution—a reference perhaps to Wells's own mother and to her sense of Victorian propriety. But the boy dreams of the fuller life he believes wearing the suit will bring him. One moonlit night he unwraps the precious gift, dons it, and in an ecstasy of fulfillment, plunges into what was, by day, a duck-pond but which to his enchanted night-sense "was a great bowl of silver moonshine . . . amidst which the stars were netted in tangled reflections of the brooding trees upon the bank" (p. 138).

The scene is suggestive of a familiar imagery in Wells: a "darkling" forest (*darkling*, almost Wells's favorite word, occurs countless times in his books and finally in the title of his penultimate novel) is bent on consuming the wanderer but is capable of being cleared by dint of superior guidance. To the boy's starry eyes, his suit equips him for his journey; but next morning his body is found in the bottom of a stone pit, "with his beautiful clothes a little bloody, and foul and stained with the duckweed from the

pond [but] his face . . . of such happiness . . . that you would
have understood indeed . . . he had died happy . . ." (p. 139).

W. Warren Wager, in the finest recent study of the ideas of
Wells, sees in the fatal passion of a small boy for fine clothes and
for moonlight a transparent parable of the perils of *ars pro arte*.[15]
Certainly it and its more famous sister story, "The Door in the
Wall," reflect unmistakably an ambivalence in Wells that fame
and status never dispelled.

In "The Door in the Wall," written in 1906, three years before
"The Beautiful Suit," Wells's little boy has grown up. He is Lionel
Wallace, a cabinet minister and an early foreshadowing of the ill-
fated politician Remington in *The New Machiavelli*. Wallace's
misgivings are less realistic than Remington's. He is haunted by a
childhood memory of a door that leads into a garden containing
all the things success has denied him—peace, delight, beauty.
Three times Wallace rejects the door before yielding to its promise
and, at the end, falls to his death, like the boy in "The Beautiful
Suit," but in an excavation pit.

The story was written at a time when a widening of the author's
social experience and meteoric rise in earnings must have produced uncertainty about the direction of his literary career or, to
use the word Wells borrows from Jung, about his multiple per-
sonas. His first marriage had failed, and his second one, while
made tenable by an understanding that he would always be free
to pursue extra-marital relationships, was never entirely satisfactory.[16] Only a few years earlier Wells could write to Arnold Bennett that the *Strand Magazine* paid one hundred twenty-five
pounds for a short story and *Pearson's* fifteen pounds a thousand
words to serialize *The Sea Lady* (1901).[17] Even earlier Wells was
earning rates equal to those accorded the well-established Thomas
Hardy.[18] By 1905, when *Kipps* appeared, he was being compared
to Dickens. Men on both sides of the Atlantic—literary figures as
various as Oscar Wilde, Henry James, Ambrose Bierce, and William Dean Howells—were welcoming Wells to the front rank of
young English literati.

Bernard Bergonzi, a modern student of the early Wells, while
finding it possible to draw Freudian implications from "The Door
in the Wall," is much more illuminating when he detects in the
story an allegory tied to warring natures within the writer:

The beautiful garden behind the closed door . . . can be readily taken as a symbol of the imagination, and Wallace as a projection of Wells's literary personality. At the start of his career as a writer he possessed a unique imagination, which flowed in a number of brilliantly original romances; yet after a few years he turned to realistic fiction, and then to works in which he tried to dragoon his imaginative powers for specifically didactic or pamphleteering purposes; at which the quality of his original imagination deserted him. Here, perhaps, we see the implication of the closed door, glimpsed from time to time, but never opened again. . . .[19]

III *The Mythmaker as Artist: Two Versions of "Country of the Blind"* [20]

"The Country of the Blind," the last of the stories which will be discussed, is more than Wells's finest achievement as a writer of short fiction. Of all his vast array of works, this story best states H. G. Wells's philosophical position in terms of the techniques of the literary artist. Wells's conception of the world was mystical and his hopes for it, as viewed in all his authentic novels and stories, dark. In 1904, when he wrote "The Country of the Blind," Wells had already approached the divided trail. Perhaps there is not in the entire history of world literature a comparable instance of a major writer who in one year produced both an epic to the position that man is a glorious creature of whims and fallibility and a classical blueprint aimed at showing that what man *is* is secondary to what mystical faith can induce him to *become*. In that year —1905—a few months after writing "The Country of the Blind," Wells erected huge literary signposts to mark both paths: for the humanist in him there was *Kipps;* for the visionary, *A Modern Utopia.*

What probably tipped the scales toward books like *Utopia* over books like *Kipps* was a destructive Fabian interlude—discussed fully in Chapter VI—which led Wells to see humanity less and less in terms of the individual and more and more in collective terms. His first essay for the Fabian Socialists was written about the same time as "The Country of the Blind." The latter is the outcry of the artist to the demands of the propagandist.

More effectively than anywhere except in certain of the scientific romances and in the last pages of *Tono-Bungay,* "The Country of the Blind" blends the riches of the humanist storyteller and the mystic visionary. To the mythmaker at the heart of Wells, no imagery proved so obsessive as that of this story. From his student days under T. H. Huxley down to his deathbed conviction that mankind had played itself out, Wells viewed mankind darkly: as a giant struggling in an evolutionary whirl to achieve a millennium of happiness and beauty, but always forced back into some sealed-off country of the blind.

Essentially, the story is a pessimistic restatement of Plato's Allegory of the Cave. The mountaineer Núñez comes unawares on a fastness deep in the Andes, where for centuries the inhabitants have been sightless and where the idea of seeing has disappeared. At first, Núñez brazenly assumes the truth of the proverb, "In the country of the blind, the one-eyed man is king" and he confidently expects to become master. However, he finds that the blind inhabitants have developed other faculties; that in a land where no one sees, the sighted are actually handicapped. Eventually Núñez is forced to submit and his submission includes giving up his eyes, regarded by the blind as grievous and useless appendages. As Núñez rebels and endeavors to escape over the mountains, he is obliged to leave behind the woman, Medina-saroté, he has come to love.

Like the prisoners of the cave, the blind have made the remote valley a symbol of estrangement. They can no more conceive of a world outside their valley than the chained cave-dwellers of Plato could imagine anything beyond the flickering shadows on the wall. Their mental inertia—and Wells wrote in a score of novels that bondage to empty tradition is the earmark of the uneducated mind—becomes apparent in the first dialogue between the newcomer and the blind:

"And you have come into the world?" asked Pedro.
"*Out* of the world. Over the mountains and glaciers; right over above there, half-way to the sun. Out of the great big world that goes down, twelve days' journey to the sea."
They scarcely seemed to heed him. "Our fathers have told us men may be made by the forces of nature," said Correa. "It is the warmth of things and moisture and rottenness—rottenness." (p. 171)

The opposition between light and darkness—truth and superstition—is nowhere more forcefully depicted than in the contrast between the sighted Núñez and the unseeing: "They told him there were indeed no mountains at all, but that the end of the rocks where the llamas grazed was indeed the end of the world; thence sprang a cavernous roof of the universe, from which the dew and the avalanches fell; and when he maintained stoutly the world had neither roof nor end as they supposed, they said his thoughts were wicked" (p. 177). And later: "Núñez had an eye for all beautiful things, and it seemed to him that the glow upon the snowfields and glaciers that rose about the valley on every side was the most beautiful thing he had ever seen" (p. 187).

The glow of the greater world that wreathed the narrow valley was, metaphorically, H. G. Wells's challenge to the unnameable hordes of humanity content to live in their determinist furrows. Even in *Kipps,* a triple-decker novel seemingly written by another part of the mind which produced "The Country of the Blind," Wells is preoccupied by the imagery of sight and shadow: "As I think of [Kipps and Ann] lying unhappily there in the darkness, my vision pierces the night. See what I can see. Above them, brooding over them . . . there is a monster . . . like all that is darkening and heavy and obstructive. . . . It is matter and darkness, it is the anti-soul, it is the ruling power of this land, Stupidity. My Kippses live in its shadow" (p. 415).

However, it is not Núñez's fate, as it was Wells's lifelong dream, to save the country of the blind from its torpor of ignorance. Rather, he is subjugated by the sightless hordes; humiliated by them; and, though he escapes the valley, defeated. The vanquishing of the spirit of independence by a conformist social order was detailed fully in Wells's early landmark of anti-utopian fiction, *When the Sleeper Wakes* (1899). Chapter IX deals more fully with the debt owed to Wells by such anti-utopians as Huxley, Orwell, and Zamiatin.

Professor Bergonzi finds in "The Country of the Blind" a mythical anticipation of the brainwashing techniques of modern totalitarianism.[21] Núñez, driven by hunger and sleeplessness and despair, agrees to conform to the blind rationale. His final surrender comes when he reluctantly agrees to the condition of his blind overlords that he allow "those irritant bodies"—his eyes—to be removed by surgery. Núñez, however, rebels at the prospect of blindness, begs his lover Medina-saroté to flee the valley with him, is refused, and dies, a worthless outcast. Meanwhile the blind world goes on, self-satisfied.

A revealing postscript to "The Country of the Blind"—indeed, to Wells's brief phase as fulltime literary artist—was provided a third of a century after his original writing of the story. In 1939, the Golden Cockerell Press of London, for a limited and numbered edition (280 copies), asked Wells to update his famous story. But, to grasp the significance of what Wells did to his finest effort in short fiction, it is necessary to jump ahead briefly. By 1939 Wells's voice had grown shrill with warnings which the world, it appeared, had failed to heed. The same year that he revised "The Country of the Blind," he had made his last voyage to the United States. His pleas for a world state were heard by thousands with the respect due an elder statesman of letters. W. Somerset Maugham recalled the twilight phase in a memoir[22] which concludes: "[Wells] was mortified that people looked upon him as a has-been. . . . When they listened it was . . . with the indulgence you accord to an old man who has outlived his interest." The world in 1939, even as the Andean valley reincarnated by Wells, *was* cracking.

The revision of "The Country of the Blind" runs parallel to the original until the final page when Núñez, having made his escape, sees along the vast rock a fresh scar. As certain of coming doom as his creator in his own agonizing last years, Núñez contemplates risking his life by returning to the valley. He considers falling at the feet of the blind people; pleading "Believe in my vision. Sometimes such an idiot as I can *see*." Only the sight of a moving crack of disaster spurs him to action. Wells describes the sound of destruction as "like the shot of a gun that starts a race." The metaphor is vintage of the man who described humanity's race between education and catastrophe.

In a tacked-on epilogue, Wells reveals that Núñez and his beloved Medina-saroté won the race. They lived to tell their tale—among Núñez's people. Wells concludes on an ironic though not surprising note for a writer who soon afterward, under sentence of death in a mortal illness, would view the seeing world as "going clean out of existence, leaving not a wrack behind. . . ."[23] Wells switches focus to Medina-saroté, now the mother of four. Her life saved by her husband's vision, she expresses no desire to see. Her last words are also the revised version's last: "The loveliness of *your* world is a complicated and fearful loveliness and mine is simple and near. . . . It may be beautiful . . . but it must be terrible to *see*." Wells appears to be saying that blindness is the only bearable antidote to the coming catastrophe. He has reversed Plato's allegory by letting one of the prisoners of the cave (or valley of the blind) return from the light—unchanged. While Medina-saroté may not have *seen*, she knows sight saved her life; yet she still prefers the illusions of the cave—blindness.

The contrast between the two versions of his most well-known short story tells more about the fatal ambivalence in Wells than can be learned from the millions of words of hack journalism that occupied him during the fallow half of an intensely productive literary live. That Wells should at the end of his life go back to one of the acknowledged minor classics of his golden period and rewrite it to conform to a growing misanthropy is one more index to the truth that he failed to resolve the conflicting claims of the artist and the public educator. Although he flawed his imperishable story, he also provided undeniable evidence at the eleventh hour that his dark conception of the world—the conception that pervaded *The Time Machine* and *The Island of Dr. Moreau*— could no longer sustain the optimism of his journalism and would, in the end, overwhelm him.

CHAPTER 5

"Spiritual Guttersnipe": The Comic Novels

CRITICS are right who see the early H. G. Wells as firmly in the tradition of the "angry young men." [1] It could not be otherwise. His childhood had been shattered by the cruelty of Victorian society which seemed bent on relegating him to the trash-heap of drapery. A rebel's attitude, or a criminal's, was the concomitant. However, in the case of Wells, an early sense of the absurd in his relationship to society was wedded to a sustaining stoicism in the face of one illness after another. This special alchemy transmuted his anger into warmly sympathetic characterizations like those of Polly and Kipps.

Wells had already filtered his warnings to a somnambulant bourgeoisie through his scientific imagination; they took the forms of time-travelling and invisibility, possibilities of human development amidst the common lot. Now it remained for him to turn from the nightmares inherent in contemporary science to those inherent in the human condition. From the start, Wells had refused to give in to the twin traumata of his youth: his father's insolvency and the draper's trade. If the greater world outside the tradesman's shop would not admit him willingly, he would force his way:

But when a man has once broken through the paper walls of everyday circumstance . . . he has made a discovery. If the world does not please you *you can change it* altogether. You may change it to something appalling, but it may be you will change it to something brighter, something more agreeable, and at worst something much more interesting. There is only one sort of man who is absolutely to blame for his own misery, and that is the man who finds life dull and dreary. . . .

This quotation sounds like the later Wells and like one of those exhortative tracts that always promised a pot of gold if only society would legislate a rainbow. Instead, it comes from Wells's most enduring novel. Appearing as it did near the end of *The History of Mr. Polly* (1910),[2] it spurred that dyspeptic little man to "clear out": to leave the shop he despised, his bed and his snoring wife Miriam; to strike out against the petty middle-class world he had accepted without question.

With the appearance of *Kipps* and *Mr. Polly*, Wells was hailed as a new Dickens. Some of the similarities may be noted. Dickens kept up a relentless attack on Marshalsea Prison where his debtor father languished; Wells during his best period held the terrain of the small tradesman as his true north and harangued at the cage which enslaved his spirit. Wells celebrated his father in Mr. Polly, just as Dickens did his in Mr. Micawber. Both writers gloried in what E. M. Forster calls, without disparagement, "flat" characterizations in which habits of speech and dress are stockpiled.[3]

However, in their feelings about the relationship of the individual to society, the differences between Dickens and Wells are more revealing than any likenesses. Dickens insisted that all it took for the world to become better would be for the Uriah Heeps and Merdles to be better people. Wells discounted individual evil —there are almost no villains in his novels—and insisted that what people *did* in society was vital. After all, had not science and his talent for it delivered him? For Dickens, workers and society would flourish if everyone behaved like Tiny Tim. For Wells, it was the organization of society that, if it did not corrupt, certainly paralyzed men from making the proper use of themselves. Dickens loved—or hated—the objects of his inspired caricatures; but Wells acknowledged late in his life what all but a select few of his books bespoke: "For all my desire to be interested I have to confess that for most things and people I don't care a damn." [4] When Dickens exalted goodness and gave Heep his "comeuppance," the sparks flew; he cared. As Wells intruded more and more directly on the actions of his novels, his voice drowned out the individuality of his characters. If he cared at all about the Britlings and Clissolds—those repositories for Wells's later thrashings with his persona—his feelings were concentrated on the fidelity with which *they* represented *him*.

But for a brief time—the period placed by Orwell between the publication of *The Time Machine* (1895) and that of *Mr. Polly*

(1910)Wells did care for the figures in his tableau. If fortune denied him that wide sympathy for humankind that placed a Dickens or a Balzac in the first rank of novelists, Wells unquestionably caught in a handful of early comic novels enough of the poetry of the human spirit to move Norman Nicholson, despite his disappointment with the later books, to proclaim that Kipps and Mr. Polly "have in them more of the stuff which endures than the characters of any of Wells's contemporaries or successors." [5]

I Kipps (1905)

It is true that Kipps and Polly—as well as Hoopdriver, Wells's bicycling draper's assistant who in *The Wheels of Chance* (1896) rode ahead—are no less projections of Wells than the writers, scientists, politicians, and teachers of the later idea-novels. These three are the products of Wells's temperament—egotistic and romantic—before it battled for its life with an intellect which tried to persuade him that the egotistic and romantic had to go.[6] Hoopdriver, Kipps, and Polly all struggle against the imperfections of the human condition that pose also as defects of Victorian society. Implicit in their dreams of a tradesman's Elysium are the pangs of the angry young sociologist in Wells. But the novelist's insights that have enshrined Kipps and Polly in the permanent gallery of memorable characters worked as minutely and as unseen in the early Wells as the zeal to preach loomed large in the later.

Artie Kipps and Mr. Polly are specimens of the muddled inferior material with which the subsequent Wells, or any other sociological messiah, would have to deal in reworking society. Although never intrusive, the autobiographical tendency in Wells is unmistakable. *Kipps,* especially in its early scenes, borrows incidents Wells had experienced as a draper, as well as childhood impressions Wells later recorded in his autobiography. The first chapter, a brilliant précis of the massive first third of the "big" novel, *Tono-Bungay,* due to be started the next year, is an account of the circumstances which thwarted a lower-middle-class youth at the end of Victoria's reign:

When Kipps left New Romney, with a small yellow tin box, a still smaller portmanteau, a new umbrella, and a keepsake half-sixpence, to become a draper, he was a youngster of fourteen, thin, with whimsical drakes' tails at the poll of his head, smallish features, and eyes that were sometimes very light and sometimes very dark, gifts those of his birth; and by the nature of his training he was indistinct in his speech, confused in his mind, and retreating in his manners. Inexorable fate had appointed him to serve his country in commerce, and the same national bias towards private enterprise and leaving bad alone, which had left his general education to Mr. Woodrow, now indentured him firmly into the hands of Mr. Shalford of the Folkestone Drapery Bazaar. (p. 34)

At this point Wells has changed little but the names of people and places. Kipps's story after he left the drapery has nothing in common with that of Wells, yet the author's presence is felt in several later chapters. He breaks in on the narrative, airs a grievance, prods with a criticism. The personal note is discernible in many places, especially in the discourses on Socialism and the housing problem.[7]

Bertie Wells saved himself from the Emporium by scholastic brilliance leading to a series of science scholarships; but Kipps is ordinary and after seven years' apprenticeship only the swift stroke of fictional incident can save him. He comes into a fortune —twenty-six thousand pounds left him by his paternal grandfather. The gift comes on the heels of a riotous drinking scene which has resulted in Kipps being dismissed by Mr. Shalford.

Under the guidance of Chester Coote, the nouveau riche Kipps joins Folkestone high society and marries Helen Walsingham, who belongs to a county family and is related to an earl. Kipps, a sadly displaced person among the upper crust, perseveres; he pretends to accept standards he knows to be false. But finally, in desperation, he runs off with his childhood sweetheart, Ann, now a Folkestone housemaid. Eventually he marries Ann, and they set up house. The path of the second marriage is rough, strewn with ludicrous quarrels over the propriety of receiving and returning "calls." In *Kipps* Wells deals superficially with problems of marriage and remarriage that he later treated in detail in a long series of novels beginning with *Love and Mr. Lewisham* (1900) and ending with *Apropos of Dolores* (1938).

In *Kipps*, Wells's verve is unimpaired, but his imagination is not nearly so rich and varied as in the scientific romances. When Artie Kipps loses his fortune—speculated away by his first wife's lawyer brother—Wells turns to the dangers of free enterprise in the hands of incompetents like Kipps, a theme he was to pursue much more memorably in *Tono-Bungay*.

Another stroke, a second fortune stemming from an investment, saves Artie and Ann. By now Kipps has recognized his place, and the money makes no change in him. In a sense the System has triumphed over Kipps. American critics, Ingvald Raknem reports, characterized the novel as disagreeable: "The appalling vulgarity of English lower-class society, its absolute aloofness from everything that gives a spiritual meaning to life, its utter imperviousness to ideas of any kind, are the impressions that chiefly remain after reading *Kipps*." [8]

What has vindicated the novel for later critics, especially when viewed in the perspective of Wells's gradual alienation from his characters, is the involvement of the author in Kipps's uneasy subservience, his clumsy, though essentially true-to-life, gropings toward self-realization:

> "Artie," said Ann.
> He woke up and pulled a stroke. "What?" he said.
> "Penny for your thoughts, Artie."
> He considered. "I really don't think I was thinking of anything," he said at last with a smile. "No." He still rested on his oars. "I expect," he said, "I was just thinking what a Rum Go everything is. I expect it was something like that."
> "Queer old Artie!"
> "Aren't I? I don't suppose there ever was a chap quite like me before." (p. 450)

As long as Wells, the man and the novelist, maintained Kipps at the center of his being, there is no danger of the sage overrunning that which in Wells was supremely ordinary. But, along with his identification with Kipps, there is a restless current of proprietary condescension. It is as if the coming giant Wells were giving the tiny Wells—Kipps—a pitying pat on the head and turning from the Kippses and Anns, with whom his romantic temperament was in perfect correspondence, to the collective forces of society, to which his restless intellect was urgently being summoned: ". . . I think of [Kipps and Ann] lying unhappily there in the darkness. . . . Above them . . . a monster . . . it is the antisoul, it is the ruling power of this land, Stupidity. My Kippses live in its shadow" (p. 415).

This statement, from near the end of *Kipps,* charts the course of H. G. Wells. He will engage the monster of Victorian stupidity in mortal combat. He will bring, as no other writer of his time, a sense of liberation to his generation. He will, as C. E. M. Joad put it, "take the wrappings off the lay figures of Victorian respectability, pass through their ribs the rapier of [his] wit." [9] And he will, in the process, sell his birthright as an artist.

II   The History of Mr. Polly (*1910*)

The History of Mr. Polly represents an advance in Wells's Cockney hero. Polly is more vigorous, both in his dreams and in his rebellion, than Kipps. If Kipps was the Wells that might have been without the latter's burning desire to cut a figure in the world, Polly is more like Bertie's father, Joseph Wells, who stargazed and dreamed of a better life. The elder Wells never rose out of the mire of his class and trade. Polly does.

Mr. Polly is Thurber's Walter Mitty carried to the tenth power —or millionth. He dreams like Mitty, but he also speaks in a frantically rebellious series of fractured "suffixiations" of incomprehensible enchantment: "Sesquippledan verboojuice" is his rendering of something he invoked in the hope that his lingual ignorance would be taken for whim. "In *Mr. Polly*," writes Vincent Brome, "Wells was . . . in the full-blooded Dickens tradition, rebelling against the frustrations of the human personality . . . kicking hard at the dumb elephant of education, but possessed more than anything with the essence of Polly, the man as a man." [10]

Wells begins his novel squarely in the middle. Mr. Polly is thirty-seven—a miserable, hopeless man—suffering from a severe attack of indigestion. In his later, more urgent concept-novels, Wells rarely delayed the rush of ideas to describe a character in the throes of dyspepsia. In his description of Mr. Polly, Wells showed a real knowledge of the details of life, the needs and troubles of the poor. After Mr. Polly endures his lot for fifteen years, he revolts. He intends to commit suicide and to burn his house down, thus providing his wife Miriam with a double insurance. The suicide does not come off but the fire is a great success, spreading from Mr. Polly's own shop to half a dozen other establishments.

Excited by his own handiwork, he gallantly rescues an old woman and becomes the town's hero.

Then Polly quietly sneaks away. For his wife, even on his wedding day, Polly has felt "alarm, desire, affection, respect—and a queer element of reluctant dislike" (p. 133). She becomes after marriage limply unhelpful, utterly irritating, perpetually ready to scold. Mr. Polly, after his "bit of arson," knows Miriam has her insurance money. He means to have life. He is a born romantic, a poet forced by miseducation to disregard every known turn of language. When a poet is forced by circumstances to spend his days in a ridiculous little shop, fighting bankruptcy without the faintest chance of avoiding ultimate defeat, one has all the elements of human tragedy.

H. G. Wells was to devote himself increasingly to what, in a few years after *Mr. Polly* was published, he would call his "Open Conspiracy" for mankind. Disillusioned by World War I, he would look at men in the collective sense; the individual human soul would hold less and less fascination for the artist moving away from Dickens and toward Shaw. A Max Beerbohm cartoon depicts H. G. Wells astride the world as if master of its fate. Wells, at the end of his tether, was to find the universe unwieldly to hold. But that most lasting contribution of a less worldly Wells —Mr. Polly—did indeed master a universe: his own fate.

Polly's rebellion was particularly well thought out and particularly wholehearted. He meant to gain his freedom and was unaffected by the fact that arson is a crime. Few readers, then or now, would condemn Mr. Polly's desertion of his wife, his deceit in allowing her to think he was drowned, or the preliminary arson. Wells was always an advocate of marshalling action to alter intolerable circumstances. The salvaging of Mr. Polly justified the means: a disconnected dyspeptic became a contented, healthy man.

But what of Miriam? What of the wife whom he abandoned? When Polly skips off, she is able to use the insurance to set up a teashop (in the variant from life, Wells established his first wife in the laundry business). Polly's rationale includes this "ode" to the folly of trying to bridge irreconcilable connubial interests: "It isn't what we try to get that we get, it isn't the good we think we do that is good. What makes us happy isn't our trying, what makes others happy isn't our trying. There's a sort of character people like and stand for and a sort they won't. You got to work it out and take the consequences" (p. 279).

All the characters in *Mr. Polly* are comic, and they are real. Among Polly's relatives is the wise Uncle Penstemon who classes his dreamer nephew as "the marrying sort":

"You *got* to get married," said Uncle Penstemon resuming his discourse. "That's the way of it. Some has. Some hain't. I done it long before I was your age. It hain't for me to blame you. You can't 'elp being the marrying sort any more than me. It's nat-ral—like poaching or drinking or wind on the stummick. You can't 'elp it and there you are. As for the good of it, there ain't no particular good in it as I can see. It's a toss-up. The hotter come the sooner cold; but they all gets tired of it sooner or later. (p. 148)

The exuberance of the book is Dickensian, yet it is without a trace of the plodding booby-traps of syntax that slow that master's novels for the modern reader. Much of Wells has dated, but not a paragraph of *Polly*. The novel is, as Sinclair Lewis wrote in 1941, as contagious as ever, "the eternal story of the kindly, friendly Little Man, whose heart and courage would anywhere . . . lift him from behind the counter of the Gents' Furnishings Shoppe, and lead him out to find a wayside world that is perpetually new and surprising." [11]

With Mr. Polly, Sidney Dark reminds the reader, Wells proved himself seer enough to realize that "tragedy and comedy are all to be found on everyone's doorstep [and they] jostle each other wherever two or three men are gathered together." [12] However, this truism H. G. Wells all too quickly forgot.

CHAPTER 6

Wells at the Crossroads

THE great crisis in Wells's life as a literary artist and as a man came neither in his thirties nor in his sixties. For H. G. Wells, the divided trail came in his early forties when, with thirty volumes already published and status as a public figure well in hand, he chose the Shavian preference, classically expressed in the preface to *Man and Superman*, to be a force recognizable only in one's own time.[1] The body of work produced by Wells before his forty-fifth year was, as Orwell has pointed out, the fruit of a first-rate literary talent. It was not accompanied, however, by even a jot of reverence for the life of the conscious literary personage visioning immortality.

Mrs. Humphry Ward wrote to Henry James that she found Wells "coarse," and James wrote back that he liked H. G.'s "cheek," a word admirably describing Wells's attitude toward the canons of art James held sacrosanct.[2] Wells's writings are replete with satirical comment on the pretensions of the literati. The vein began with one of his earliest pieces, an essay (contributed in 1893 to the *Pall Mall Gazette*) suggesting that literary capacity is engendered by indigestion and proposing that chemical food be exploited for its unwholesomeness and salutary effect on literary aspirants.[3] Wells's penchant for ridiculing the pompous solemnity of the artist was climaxed in 1911 with the publication of *Boon* and its famous burlesque of the manner of Henry James. A James novel, he wrote, "is like a church lit but without a congregation to distract you, with every light and line focused on the high altar. And on the altar, very reverently placed, intensely there, is a dead kitten, an egg shell, a bit of string" (p. 455). Wells's badinage against the literati was largely defensive; it was prompted by their patronization of him "to the limit of endurance." The extent to which criticism wounded him can best be gauged by his tendency for the next thirty years to strike back at what he took to be an irresponsible campaign to bury him as a novelist of stature.[4]

Ironically, the angry young man was digging his own grave faster than his foes of the establishment. Wells's self-interment began in 1903 when he was invited by Beatrice and Sidney Webb and Bernard Shaw to join forces with the London Fabian Society. His acceptance did more than any single act to seal his fate. Although there are many tributes to Wells's influence on the Fabians —a longtime secretary of the group called *New Worlds for Old,* written by Wells while a member of the Fabian Executive, the best recent book on English Socialism[5]—the five-year interlude was destructive to both the creative artist and the man. Although Wells railed at their parochialism and left them finally over a dispute with old guard members about methods of expanding their influence, he involved himself in a long series of intramural squabbles that continually deflected his aim from more primary matters in the life of a novelist of widening scope.

When the showdown came, Wells was soundly thrashed in parliamentary debate. Shaw, who led the onslaught, later declared that he smote down his inexperienced adversary to save Wells later embarrassment, as well as to protect the reputations of some of the older Fabians whom Wells had maligned. Shaw, who was intensely competitive and could not have helped but recognize the arrival of an equal, summarized the interlude by saying that the Old Gang did not extinguish Wells; he annihilated himself.[6] In after years, while never quite forgiving Shaw for what he regarded as a needlessly prominent role in his discreditation, Wells confessed that his frustrations in the Fabian Society reinforced his bias against all human planners.[7] He later embraced enthusiastically and then violently rejected, in their turn, the Labor Party, the League of Nations, and the Soviet Union.

No artist ever gave more of himself to the issues of his day. However, his panaceas were invariably visionary by-products of his creativity. In a recent issue of *Commentary,* Leonard Woolf tells an amusing story about how badly Wells took the words of a critic that he did his thinking with his imagination.[8] Of Wells, no truer words were ever spoken. Those of his ideas that are remembered at all were given fire by his imagination. He would in a few years embark on his mammoth *Outline of History* as an indefatigable lobbyist for a World State. Yet nothing of that gigantic scheme to sell an idea survives with the vividness of those end-of-world scenes in *The Time Machine,* whose first version was penned by an unknown science student. Membership in the Fabians forced Wells to formulate endless "what-I-believe" slogans uncongenial to the intuitive artist.

I First and Last Things (*1908*)

Out of the welter of essays stemming from the Fabian phase (the title of his first excursion, "The Questions of Scientific Administrative Areas in Relation to Municipal Undertakings," gives an idea of what the Fabians put him up to) came *First and Last Things,* Wells's most fruitful effort at a systematic statement of his philosophy. As early as 1891, Wells had written an article for Frank Harris and the *Fortnightly Review* called "The Rediscovery of the Unique." Now, fifteen years later, Wells reiterated his denial of scientific precision as possible in questions of human relations:

Now I make my beliefs as I want them. I do not attempt to distil them out of fact as physicists distil their laws. I make them thus and not thus exactly as an artist makes a picture so and not so. I believe that is how we all make our beliefs, but that many people do not see this clearly and confuse their beliefs with perceived and proven fact. . . .

The artist cannot defend his expression as a scientific man defends his, and demonstrate that they are true upon any assumptions whatsoever. . . .

. . . I adopt certain beliefs because I feel the need for them, because I feel an often quite unanalyzable rightness in them. . . . My belief in them rests upon the fact that they work for me and satisfy my desire for harmony and beauty. They are arbitrary assumptions, if you will, that I see fit to impose upon my universe. (pp. 216–17)

This credo, of course, is that of the artist, whatever his medium. From this position there should follow, as a freshet flows from a mainstream, a disposition to regard each human, the raw material for literary art, as unique. However, following a statement of belief that so befits the creator of a Kipps and a Mr. Polly, Wells swerved from the acceptance of individuality as uniqueness to a belief in a super-human synthesis transcending and absorbing individuality:

> The essential fact in man's history to my sense is the slow unfolding of a sense of community with his kind, of the possibilities of co-operations leading to scarce dreamt-of collective powers, of a synthesis of the species, of the development of a common general idea, a common general purpose out of a present confusion. In that awakening of the species, one's own personal being lives and moves—a part of it and contributing to it. *One's individual existence is not so entirely cut off as it seems at first; one's entirely separate individuality is another, a profounder, among the subtle inherent delusions of the human mind. . . .*
>
> You see that from this point of view . . . our individualities, our nations and states and races are but bubbles and clusters of foam upon the great stream of the blood of the species, incidental experiments in the growing knowledge and consciousness of the race. (pp. 248–50)

Although Wells anticipated and denied the charge that his statement was mystical, it is difficult to reconcile the Mind-of-Race with the minds of those raw, lower-middle-class types whose chronicles were building Wells a solid reputation as a novelist of power. It was clear that in *First and Last Things* H. G. Wells was formulating a rationale for the kind of art to which he planned to devote himself. In 1911 he would astonish the literary establishment with his emancipation proclamation for the Novel. "We [novelists] are going to write," he declared, "about the whole of human life . . . about business and finance and politics and precedence and pretentiousness and decorum and indecorum, until a thousand pretenses and ten thousand impostures shrivel in the cold, clear air of our elucidations." [9] Wells's credo, as both philosopher and novelist, should have presented fair warning of the spate of "dialogue" and "idea" novels that were to come from his pen.

However, at about the same time—1906—that he was writing Fabian drafts of the essays later revised into *First and Last Things*, Wells set to work on an ambitious novel upon the accepted lines. It occupied him for nearly three years, a one-book

effort unmatched in his career. *Tono-Bungay* found Wells thinking the only way he found congenial—with his imagination.
Certainly, with the highest expression his art could summon, he
wrestled with the dilemma implicit in *First and Last Things:* the
intellect of the man trained in science versus the intuition of the
man fitted by nature to be an artist. When, in 1922, Wells prepared
special prefaces for the twenty-eight-volume Atlantic Edition of
his works, he acknowledged that, with one exception, "it is far
truer to call [my books] Journalism than Art." [10] That exception
was the novel he called *Tono-Bungay*.

II   Tono-Bungay (*1909*)

Tono-Bungay deserves a place on bookshelves within the genre
Frierson calls the "life-novel." [11] It merits mention in the same
breath as Samuel Butler's *Way of All Flesh,* Romain Rolland's
Jean Christophe, Somerset Maugham's *Of Human Bondage,* and
D. H. Lawrence's *Sons and Lovers.* Like them, Wells's novel may
best be described, as Geoffrey West has said, as "thought-
adventure." [12] Its hero, George Ponderevo—like Christophe, Philip
Carey, and Paul Morel—is the personification of the intellectual
consciousness which seeks a reality to stand against all its tests.
Again and again this hero makes a crucible of every level and
phase of society, and always life crowds in on him. The novel
combines to advantage, therefore, the three strains for which
Wells is noted: the spokesman for a generation escaping from
Victorianism; the scientific romancer who brought the Fourth Dimension and air-machine travel to the semi-educated man who
had never heard of Einstein or Bleriot; and the portrayer of warm
human characters in the manner of, though with distinct differences from, Dickens. Few British novels present with comparable
vividness the heralding of the new century amidst the debris of
the old. Perhaps Ford Madox Ford's *Parade's End* is the only saga
comparable to *Tono-Bungay* in this transitional way. The ordinary nineteenth-century novel seems to present an apparently
static society with only an undercurrent of dissatisfaction and tur-
moil, and the twentieth-century novel shows a society whose institutions are often wholly discredited and disrupted. *Tono-Bungay*
—and the Ford tetralogy, which came some years later—stand
half-way between these two. Wells portrays the disruption of

moral values in the hands of a corrupt get-rich-quick tycoon; Ford shows how World War I completed the disruption of British society.

The first third of *Tono-Bungay*, a fictionalized transcript of the opening (and best) chapters of *Experiment in Autobiography*, sends George Ponderevo, an intellectualized Kipps, through a Victorian grotesquerie compounded of adolescent love and servants' gossip. The partners in this story are George Ponderevo, son of a maidservant, and Beatrice, a niece of the lady of the house. The love scenes in *Tono-Bungay* bear a striking resemblance to those in *Kipps*, which preceded it, and in *Mr. Polly*, which followed. Invariably the object of George's heart's desire (or Artie Kipps's or Alfred Polly's) is viewed as on a pedestal. It is revelatory how much these scenes—the only convincing love scenes Wells ever wrote—are alike in this vertical sense. In the following quotation George, from the vantage of success and scandal, is recalling the time he, at fourteen, first kissed and embraced Beatrice:

I recall something of one talk under the overhanging bushes of the shrubbery—I on the park side of the stone wall, and the lady of my worship a little inelegantly astride thereon. Inelegantly, do I say? You should have seen the sweet imp as I remember her. Just her poise on the wall comes suddenly clear before me, and behind her the light various branches of the bushes of the shrubbery that my feet might not *profane*, and far away and high behind her, dim and stately, the cornice of the great facade of Bladesover rose against the dappled sky. (p. 41)

"Profane" is italicized because it is crucial to Wells's idealizing of the love relationship between his heroes and heroines. George Ponderevo, coarse son of a servant, and Kipps and Polly, bumpkins both, but redeemed by an inner poetry, fear they *profane* the women they covet. It was also the word Henry James, undoubtedly without intent to wound the socially maladjusted Wells, used to describe the manner in which Wells handled a love scene in his later novel, *Marriage*. "Profane" appears in the midst of what, to Wells, were barbs of betrayal in James's essay on Bennett, himself, and the other younger novelists. It moved Wells to lash back with *Boon*, the lampoonery of James which ended their friendship a few months before the latter's death. This, however, is not the place to take up in detail the James-Wells quarrel, a matter dealt with in Chapter Eight.

The reunion of George and Beatrice in *Tono-Bungay* comes years later. Ponderevo has seen his marriage wrecked, and his career threatened by the scandal of tono-bungay, a preposterous bottled health elixir; he is now a successful builder of battleships. But Wells's positioning of George and Beatrice in the reunion scene is unchanged from the adolescent dream. Beatrice still sits on a citadel above and beyond her partner: "At the further corner from the cedar she perched herself up upon the parapet and achieved an air of comfort among the lichenous stones. 'Now tell me,' she said, 'all about yourself. . . . I know such duffers of men. . . . You've climbed'" (p. 389). But the Wellsian hero has not climbed out of an adolescent, almost puppy-love-like relationship with his inamorata. The scene ends quickly; Beatrice is summoned away. The love object in all of Wells's early novels is unattainable. In *Kipps* the pattern recurs. Artie asks Ann if she will be his girl:

> Towards dusk that evening they chanced on one another at the gate by the church; but though there was much in his mind, it stopped there with a resolute shyness until he and Ann were out of breath catching cockshafers. . . . Ann sat up upon the gate, dark against vast masses of flaming crimson and darkling purple, and her eyes looked at Kipps from a shadowed face. There came a stillness between them and quite abruptly he was moved to tell his love.
> "Ann," he said, "I *do* like you. I wish you was my girl. . . . I say, Ann: will you *be* my girl?" (p. 26)

She consents but, as in *Tono-Bungay*, the hero must try and fail in a first marriage (the fate, too, of his creator) and learn that the nouveau riche need more than money to break through the bastille of the Victorian class structure. In *The History of Mr. Polly*, Polly is prevented by a wall from fulfillment. Here in a first meeting between Polly and Christabel, the latter stares down at the undersized stranger as

> she sought to estimate his social status on her limited basis of experience. He stood leaning with one hand against the wall, looking up at her and tingling with daring thoughts. He was a littleish man, you must

remember, but neither mean-looking nor unhandsome in those days.
. . . He had an inspiration to simple speech that no practised trifler
with love could have bettered, "There *is* love at first sight," he said,
and said it sincerely.

She stared at him with eyes round and big with excitement.

"I think," she said slowly, and without any signs of fear or retreat,
"I ought to get back over the wall."

"It needn't matter to you," he said; "I'm just a nobody. But I know
you are the best and most beautiful thing I've ever spoken to." His
breath caught against something. "No harm in telling you that," he
said.

"I should have to go back if I thought you were serious," she
said. . . . (p. 105)

Their idyll is—characteristically—interrupted; resumed in twenty
minutes; and interrupted again. In all, their acquaintance lasts ten
days. The abortive—the unfulfilled—adolescent male fantasy is at
the heart of the love interest in Wells's major trilogy. As mere
partners in these dreams, the women have no life of their own. It
is a measure of Wells's limitation as a novelist that, in the long
series of novels about marriage, Wells projects a *knowledge* of
women but no *feeling* for them. Remington's first wife in *The
New Machiavelli* is remembered only because of her last letter
which cuts so close to the truth of the essentially destructive nature of free love. Lady Mary emerges in *The Passionate Friends*
only as a *deus ex machina,* never with an independent identity of
her own.

The latter portions of *Tono-Bungay,* chronicling comic-serious
adventures with a fraudulent patent-medicine and with an ill-fated
search for a do-all elixir known as "quap," clearly portend the
coming age of advertising and the hard-sell. If Wells has been
rightly called the star reporter of his day, it has not been sufficiently stressed that he also understood, with a sophistication astonishing for its time, the spirit of public relations and publicity.
Wells appears always to have understood the power of the
graphic arts to sway men's minds. As early as in *The First Men in
the Moon,* it is a column of "mean little advertisements" in *Lloyd's
News* which are suspended before the earth-departing Mr. Bedford as he and Cavor ascend toward the moon.[13]

The purveyor of Tono-Bungay quackery is a bubbling sprite of an uncle, Teddy Ponderevo, who in at least two respects is a chip off his creator's block. He, like the early Wells, has escaped from pill dispensing and is an outsider storming the bastions of society. An early scene between George and his uncle is a capsule of Victorian mores under bombardment from the New Spirit which threatens the innocence of the Edwardian era:

"Well, George!" he said, quite happily unconscious of my silent criticism, "what do you think of it?"
"Well," I said, "in the first place—it's a damned swindle!"
"Tut! tut!" said my uncle. "It's as straight as—It's fair trading!"
"So much the worse for trading," I said.
"It's the sort of thing everybody does. After all, there's no harm in the stuff—and it may do good. It might do a lot of good—giving people confidence. For instance, against an epidemic. See? Why not? I don't see where your swindle comes in."
"H'm," I said. "It's a thing you either see or don't see." (pp. 177–78)

The novel, written in first-person and presented almost entirely in flashbacks, gets properly started with the introduction of Uncle Teddy. He makes his entrance as a small druggist in a dead country town. He quickly exhibits to his nephew "the temperament of a Napoleon of finance spoiling for conquest"—a meteor in the making. Teddy Ponderevo is the sort of outsider-adventurer Wells liked, although such living counterparts as Bottomley and Birkenhead, Ramsay MacDonald and Zaharoff, would wither and die among the élite bores of Wells's utopias.[14] Writing several decades before advertising magnates would begin to appear in English and American novels, Wells does not make the mistake of caricature. Ponderevo, a fraud to be sure, is never the doer of direct villainy like Merdle, that other pioneer financier of fiction, in *Little Dorrit*. Even his charlatanry is tempered by a taste for the business. He glosses over his shady dealings with such phrases as "Romance of Commerce" or "Room for Enterprise." Wells cannot avoid a kindly tolerance for Teddy, his brother in arms. But since, to the burgeoning socialist in Wells, Teddy and tono-bungay represent the dangers of irresponsible capitalism, the author employs an altogether balanced nephew to be the uncle's conscience: "You don't mean to say you think doing this stuff up in bottles and swearing it's the quintessence of strength . . . is straight?" (p. 178).

Professor Harry T. Moore, in a foreword to a recent paperback edition of the novel, properly notes that the book transports the reader to today's world of slogans that bark out at him from the TV screen. For, after Uncle Teddy scores a first success with tono-bungay, he hucksters a soap. What, continues Professor Moore's analogy, "gurgles more invitingly or foams more bewitchingly on our television screens than, respectively, patent medicines and soap?" [15] But Teddy, given the gift of high finance, as Griffin in *The Invisible Man* was given the gift of transparency, comes to a pathetic demise. Teddy threatens to disorganize the industrial fabric of England, just as Griffin bid well to destroy Iping Village. Both go beyond their depth and become menaces to be eliminated.

Tono-Bungay effectively links the comic-novel triumphs of Wells's past with the tract-novels of his next vein. For all his ambition and unscrupulousness, Teddy never loses the innocence of a Hoopdriver or of a Kipps. The fall of the Ponderevo empire, his patent-medicine sham world in bits around him, is described by Wells with a moving concern for the single human soul. Teddy's meeting with nephew George at the moment of bankruptcy brings out the finest in Wells:

I discovered that his face was wet with tears, that his wet glasses blinded him. He put up his fat hand and clawed them off clumsily, felt inefficiently for his pocket handkerchief, and then to my horror, as he clung to me, he began to weep aloud, this little, old world-worn swindler. It wasn't just sobbing or shedding tears, it was crying as a child cries—It was—oh!—terrible.

"It's cruel," he blubbered at last. "They asked me questions. They kep' asking me questions, George." (pp. 473–74)

Ponderevo's death comes ignominiously enough in a forgotten French village. More than one critic has suggested that Wells drew on memories of the deathbed vigil spent with his friend, the novelist George Gissing, to describe the poignant fade-out of a late Victorian tycoon.[16] "So ended all that flimsy inordinate stir . . . that was George Gissing," wrote Wells in a memorable but widely misunderstood epitaph for the man closest to him among fellow writers at the turn of the century.[17] With the fictional event —the death of Uncle Teddy Ponderevo—the "inordinate stir" became the meaningless "push and promotions . . . the excitements, the dinners and disputations" of the human rocket's upward thrust. Wells had deep affection for Gissing but regretted what he considered the waste of a potentially important writer who unduly depreciated life. So, too, the fictional Uncle Teddy is shown to be defeated by the failure of his lower-class, village-druggist background to equip him for the tycoon's role thrust upon him by Tono-Bungay.

   Tono-Bungay comes closest of any of the novels to being a spiritual biography; it is closer, certainly, than *William Clissold,* a catalogue of issues that occupied the world and Wells between the great wars. The last chapter of *Tono-Bungay* evokes symbolically and poetically the entire spirit of the novel. Using an ocean destroyer as his contemporary time machine—George Ponderevo has survived a trap of the new century, irresponsible capitalism, and has become a builder of great ships—Wells portrays the inexorable and explosive quality of the coming age in the wake of the vessel:

They [the ships] stand out bound on strange missions of life and death, to the killing of men in unfamiliar lands. And, now behind us is blue mystery and the phantom flash of unseen lights, and presently even these are gone, and I and my destroyer tear out to the unknown across a great grey space. We tear into the great spaces of the future and the turbines fall to talking in unfamiliar tongues. Out to the open we go, to windy freedom and trackless ways. Light after light goes down. England and the Kingdom, Britain and the Empire, the old prides and the old devotions, glide abeam, astern, sink down upon the horizon, pass —pass. The river passes—London passes, England passes. . . . (p. 528)

   Whether the destroyer is taken to be the mind of H. G. Wells or the inexorability of time itself, there is in this passage, one which closes this novel of thought-adventure, a perfect rendering of the inevitability—the glory—of change. In his mind's journey, Ponderevo (Wells) has sensed the futility of his uncle's scramble. But the way of intellect, one senses, is also found wanting; for it is powerless to chart the regions of the unknowable: "But through the confusion sounds another note. Through the confusion something drives, something that is at once human achievement and the most inhuman of all existing things. Something comes out of it. . . . How can I express the values of a thing at once so essential and so immaterial? It is something that calls upon such men as I with an irresistible appeal" (pp. 528–29). Whatever triumph Ponderevo has salvaged from the wreckage of tono-bungay, it has to do with some precious and inherent quality that welds the individual—even a virtuoso individual like Wells—to the human race.

And, at last, the closing words of the novel: "We are all things that make and pass, striving upon a hidden mission, out to the open sea." Here, again, is H. G. Wells, artist and mystic. *Tono-Bungay* becomes the dramatic, even poetic, expression of *First and Last Things*. Wells increasingly came to regard individual men as but transitory thoughts and to see the key to human evolution in the collective Mind of Race. Only in *Tono-Bungay* was Wells able to blend successfully the riches of the mystic visionary and the storyteller.

CHAPTER 7

Socialism and Sex: Samurai and Valkyries

I The New Machiavelli (*1911*)

WELLS called *The New Machiavelli* "a queer confused novel . . . one of my worst and one of my most revealing." [1] Written directly after *Tono-Bungay* and *The History of Mr. Polly,* it was less carefully wrought than the former and showed how easily the humanistic satire of the latter could be transformed into lampoonery. More than any previous work, the new novel illumined the path Wells's fiction would take for the next forty years.

George Ponderevo is reincarnated in *Machiavelli* as Remington. But, in place of the intellectual voyager, Wells ushers in the first of a long line of Wellsians—men full of good intentions and eager to rebuild the world. Remington, most of all, reveals Wells's almost Byronic self-adulation. He is a New Republican, Wells's new breed of politician-thinker, who strides forth to battle in the arena of Westminster; savors the heady potions of Socialism; imbibes its dream, but distrusts its practitioners to the point of hatred; leaves his wife; and ends in disgrace.

The novel was viewed in 1911 as a *roman à clef.* One critic remarked that *The New Machiavelli* was the book in which Wells betrayed some of his best friends.[2] Wells duly registered his objections to criticism which was "incapable of the fine but real distinction between giving a similar figure and . . . 'putting people into a book.'" [3] Nevertheless, the smoke from Wells's fiery departure from the Fabians had not yet cleared, and it was inevitable that minor characters in his political novel should be taken as models of living antagonists.

But what made *Machiavelli* one of Wells's most self-revealing books was its deeply pessimistic commentary on the chances of idealism when in conflict, not only against centuries of muddle-headed political thinking, but against irrational impulses within the idealist. Remington is defeated by his own instinct to break the law. The maker who would reform the system into a socialist Elysium is also the breaker who destroys himself by choosing a mistress instead of a career. Remington's choice gives the book a thematic unity and points out, more clearly than any other novel that Wells wrote, how little faith he actually had in the triumph of schemes that rule out existential aspects in men.

Wells depicts the world of Westminster as essentially formless. Against this sympathy for the resistance of men to order he pits the zeal for planning of Oscar and Altiora Bailey, flimsily disguised counterparts of his old Fabian friends, Sidney and Beatrice Webb: [4]

> At the Baileys' one always seemed to be getting one's hands on the very strings that guided the world. You heard legislation projected to affect this "type" and that; statistics marched by you with sin and shame and injustice and misery reduced to quite manageable percentages . . . [and] you felt you were in a sort of signal box with levers all about you, and the world outside there, albeit a little dark and mysterious beyond the window, running on its lines in ready obedience to these unhesitating lights, true and steady to trim termini.
>
> And then with all this administrative fizzle, this pseudo-scientific administrative chatter, dying away in your head, out you went into the limitless grimy chaos of London streets and squares . . . a vague incessant murmur of cries and voices, wanton crimes and accidents bawled at you from the placards . . . and you found yourself swaying back to the opposite conviction that the huge formless spirit of the world it was that held the strings and danced the puppets on the Bailey stage. (pp. 232–33)

Wells sacrifices Remington to the triumph of the "huge formless spirit" of life. The passage reveals Wells's distrust of some of man's instrumentalities as antidotes to the chaos of his condition. *The New Machiavelli,* a representative work of his middle period, echoes *The Island of Dr. Moreau* in its view of the world as "nothing but a mere heap of dust, fortuitously agitated"—the mechanistic view.[5] In the tract-novels—the planned societies—of his sterile final period, Wells assumed the stance of one who believed in inevitable progress, in an evolution in which the mind would be orderly and vital. Remington (Wells) certainly did not believe this way in 1911. Although Remington is pictured as blaming his failures in politics on a lag between his political progress (too fast) and his education (too retarded), what he is really saying is that the economic and social disorder, the incoherence and planlessness, the unequal struggle of reason with the natural energies and instincts of human life, are in large part characteristic of the way of the modern world.

The New Machiavelli, by Wells's own admission among his most "revealing" novels, is a deeply Existential work. Remington's external passion for order is at war with the irrationality at his core. The novel bares the conflicting passions which nagged H. G. Wells at forty-five. "You are always *talking* of order and system," writes Margaret to Remington a week before he left her for another woman; ". . . but by a sort of instinct you seem to want to break the law. . . . You are at once makers and rebels, you and Isabel too. You're bad people—criminal people . . . and yet full of something the world must have. . . . It may be there is no making without destruction, but . . . it is nothing but an instinct for lawlessness that drives you. . . ." (pp. 557–58) Raknem suggests that Wells probably inserted this letter at the end of the novel because he had a bad conscience.[6] Margaret's complaints are such as Jane Wells could justifiably have made. Certainly Remington's taking of a mistress could be compared to Wells's own practice before, during, and after the writing of *The New Machiavelli*. Wells reveals in his autobiography that, a few years after his second marriage, he asked to be released from his marriage vows. Arnold Bennett once noted that Wells placed photographs of three of his mistresses on his mantelpiece beside that of his wife.[7]

But Remington is more than Wellsian self-projection. He is a monument to the proposition that the world is inhabited by error-prone, passionate, jealous creatures who are given to excesses beyond their control. Remington, like Wells, would be uneasy in a world state geared to perfectibility; and Remington would as surely be banished from it as he was from Westminster. Moreover, *The New Machiavelli*, along with the below-surface insights into its author, provides revealing documentation for the political historian. Wells was among the first to show in a novel the force of education in liberalizing the minds of the political intelligentsia in Edwardian England. Men, according to Remington "are becoming increasingly constructive and selective. The past will rule them less, the future more. It is not simply party but school and college and county and country that lose their glamour. One does not hear nearly as much as our forefathers did of the 'Old Harrovian,' 'Old Arvonian,' 'Old Etonian' claim to this or that unfair advantage or unearned sympathy. . . . A widening sense of fair play destroys such things" (p. 323).

Remington assaults the world of British politics as Ponderevo did the world of commerce. He projects the enthusiasm and idealism so characteristic of his creator. He has been, unlike Wells, to Cambridge; is taken under wing by the Baileys, as Wells was sponsored by the Webbs; and joins the young Socialists, as Wells joined the Fabians and the Coefficients. Wells's grasp in this novel of the three-tiered structure of British politics is enlightening. He gives a picture of flux and chaos. The old Conservatism appeared undermined because it was joined to old Westminster traditions, and seemed not at all alive "to the greatness of the Present and to the vaster Future." The Liberals showed clearly what they were against; the trouble was to find out what on earth they were for. The third party, the Socialists, had become "a sort of big intellectual No-Man's Land." Finally, the Labor Party had a constructive program, but most of its members were hostile to education and, except for an obvious antagonism to employers and property owners, almost destitute of ideas.

The book emerges, at one level, as a rationale for Wells's lifelong inability to mesh his ideas with those of any individual or of any group. At the height of despair over the Fabians, Remington speaks for Wells and his disenchantment with British Socialists: " 'When you think of the height and depth and importance and wisdom of the Socialist ideas, and see the men who are running them. . . . A big system of ideas like Socialism grows up out of the obvious common sense of our present conditions. It's as impersonal as science. All these men—they've given nothing to it. . . . We mustn't confuse Socialism with the Socialists . . .' " (p. 342).

The novel also displays Wells as at once contemptuous of politicians and as fascinated by them. He is equally divided in his feelings about the new type of suffragette heroine epitomized by Altiora Bailey. Wells called them the "Marcella crop" after the title character of Mrs. Humphry Ward's influential novel: women who have dropped from their shoulders the Victorian draperies of timidity, false modesty, and propriety—who have rolled up their sleeves to battle for industrial and economic amelioration. Wells's picture of Altiora—a kind of intellectual Valkyrie—is cruel but not without grudging admiration:

She had much of the vigour and handsomeness of a slender impudent young man, and an unscrupulousness altogether feminine. She was one of those women who are wanting in—what is the word?—muliebrity. . . . She was entirely unfitted for her sex's sphere. She was neither uncertain, coy nor hard to please, and altogether too stimulating and aggressive for any gentleman's hours of ease. . . . Yet you mustn't imagine she was an inelegant or unbeautiful woman, and she is inconceivable to me in high collars or any sort of masculine garment. But her soul was bony, and at the base of her was a vanity gaunt and greedy! (pp. 220–21)

Interesting as Remington's observations on politics and the Baileys are to political clinicians, there is another facet to *The New Machiavelli*. It provides an early view of the rising tide of feminism and the battle of the sexes. Margaret is the first of what André Maurois calls those "half-Fabian, half-aristocratic Amazons" [8] who in one Wells novel after another join their mates in battling the class structure. Margaret's meeting with Remington, a promising young Liberal-Socialist, is arranged by Altiora Bailey. Margaret is intelligent, beautiful, idealistic; and she has enough money of her own to help him in his political career. They marry, but something clouds their married life. Despite Wells's reluctance to come to artistic grips with Lawrentian themes, he clearly intends to blame their troubles on sex. Remington describes the conflict: "My quality is sensuous and ruled by warm impulses; hers was discriminating and essentially inhibitory. I like naked bodies and the jolly smell of things. She abounded in reservations, in circumlocutions and evasions, in keenly appreciated secondary points" (p. 276).

It is impossible not to see in this novel, as in *Tono-Bungay*, a catharsis for the failure of Wells's first marriage.[9] In October, 1891, the twenty-five-year-old Wells married Isabel Mary Wells, a cousin. She insisted on a long engagement as Marion does in *Tono-*

Bungay. Once they were married, the cloud noted in *Machia-velli*—Remington's sensuality versus Margaret's reserve—darkened their relationship. Wells confessed to "an unalterable difference . . . in our nervous reactions. I felt and acted swiftly and variously and at times loosely and superficially, in the acutest contrast to her gentler and steadier flow. There was no contact nor comparison between our imaginative worlds. . . ." [10] Moreover, Remington falls in love with Isabel Rivers, just as Wells fell in love with Amy Catherine Robbins. Since it would be several years before Remington's first wife could give him a divorce, Remington runs away with Isabel. In Edwardian England, divorce for a politician was career suicide; Remington knows, therefore, that his action will ruin him.

Wells has described his desire for other women fully in this novel. So central is this sexual uneasiness to the fabric of a whole succession of Wells's novels from *Tono-Bungay* and *Machiavelli,* down to the last tired reiterations of *Babes in the Darkling Wood* thirty years later, that a recent critic, Montgomery Belgion, sees in Wells's hostility to monogamy the key to his zealousness for social reform: "As his stories show, he credited other people with no independent existence. So he could but think of himself. The one entity of which, apart from himself, he was conscious was the environment, and . . . he felt that this environment required to be 'tamed.' Having tried monogamy and found it irksome, when he saw that monogamy went on being respected in the environment, he was impelled, as part of the 'taming,' to try to get monogamy generally condemned and discarded." [11]

This view is a perceptive one, as far as it goes; but it is shortsighted. One side of Wells unquestionably saw an opportunity to convert ideas into action by living openly out of wedlock with a series of suffragettes and lady writers in London during his struggling Fabian days, and in his villa in the south of France during the 1920's and 1930's when his was one of the most famous names in the world.[12] But the line of novels that started with *The New Machiavelli* and *Ann Veronica,* both literary *causes célèbres,* has a deeper intention than advocacy of free love. They are, writes Kenneth Rexroth, "about matrimony, about the mysteries and difficulties and agonies and tragedies and—rarely—the joys of the search for a true 'life of dialogue.' " [13]

Wells had stressed as early as 1905 the need for this life of dialogue. In *A Modern Utopia,* he writes:

"A man under the Rule who loves a woman who does not follow it, must either leave the Samurai to marry her, or induce her to accept what is called the Woman's Rule, which, while it exempts her from the severer qualifications and disciplines, brings her regimen into a working harmony with his."

"Suppose she breaks the Rule afterwards?"

"He must leave either her or the order."

"There is matter for a novel or so in that."

"There has been matter for hundreds." (p. 261)

The general problem of marriage—more exactly, the relation of one individual to another—is the concern of all of Wells's longer novels. From *Love and Mr. Lewisham* in 1900 to *Babes in the Darkling Wood* in 1940, Wells wrestled with one variation after another on the theme.

Brome has said, with entire truth, that the freedom of the sexes "was first made articulate by Wells, laughingly reaffirmed by Shaw, developed in lyrical unrestraint by Lawrence, and given a cynical sanction—if not smear—by Aldous Huxley." [14] In *The New Machiavelli,* despite the tempered lampoonery of Beatrice Webb, Wells showed himself to be firmly feminist—and more. His early works developed out of a curious linking of the evolutionary zeal of T. H. Huxley, the imaginative riches of Poe and Verne, and the "flat" caricaturing of Dickens. But Wells's private code in relation to marriage and plural associations was straight out of Shelley by way of Rousseau. [15] "I was entirely out of accord with the sentimental patterns and focussed devotions adopted by most people about me," Wells writes in his autobiography. "Regardless of every visible reality about me of law, custom, social usage, economic necessities and the unexplored psychology of womanhood, I developed my adolescent fantasy of free, ambitious, self-reliant women who would mate with me and go their way, as I desired to go my way. . . ." [16] Most of Wells's heroines are charter members of this delectably unreal class of intellectual Valkyries. In his most infamous heroine he solidified his adolescent fantasy. In creating Ann Veronica, he whipped up a storm in the country that had created Mrs. Grundy.

II Ann Veronica (1909)

Ann Veronica "came like an angel of freedom, a very determined audacious angel, into the lives of endless young women"
during the second decade of the twentieth century.[17] There
was an electric reaction to this novel which called for sexual
license sixty years after Hawthorne's Hester Prynne had quietly
accepted the emblem of the scarlet letter. It was no overstatement
to say that the underlying conflict of centuries was thrust into the
open at the point in the novel where Ann Veronica announces her
intention of attending an unchaperoned dance in London and of
spending the night in a hotel, and her aunt utters that apprehen-
sive phrase, "But, my dear!"[18] In Edwardian England, girls had to
be chaperoned; none questioned the dicta of their fathers. It was
also a time when no decent girl worked for a living, expressed
political opinions publicly, or dared be seen with a suffragette.

Odette Keun, a once close friend who has expressed her disenchantment with Wells in an overwrought but perceptive memoir,
described the impact, especially on young women of her generation, of a book like *Ann Veronica*: "Into this foul and insupport-
able nightmare leapt [Wells] . . . to thrust and cut and hack
. . . at the tentacles, the octopus, the whole evil, heavy, stupid,
brutal frame in which we were imprisoned. . . . We were being
delivered."[19] For Ann Veronica, a daughter of the English middle-
class—a class which considered the Wells of 1910 to be a distinct
outsider—defies her father, flees her home to live apart, becomes
a violently partisan suffragette, and eventually throws herself into
the arms of the man she loves.

There is no way to know exactly how many daughters left home
to follow the path to fulfillment forged by Ann Veronica. Wells
said only that advanced young people in Sweden, Bulgaria, Russia, and Austria "learned to their amazement that there were
young people like themselves in England." The novel, he wrote,
was not so much criticized as attacked "with hysterical animosity
by people who did not like the heroine or who disapproved of her
thoughts and ways."[20] As a result, the book was banned by libraries and preached against by earnest clergymen. There was not
only a bad press and public denunciation but attempts to ostra-
cize Wells socially. St. Loe Strachey's diatribe is characteristic of

the criticism leveled at Wells. The novel was reprehensible, Strachey wrote, not so much because it discussed sexuality frankly but because in describing Ann Veronica sympathetically Wells was demolishing the Old Victorian standards:

The Book is based on the negation of woman's purity and of man's good faith in the relations of the sexes. It teaches, in effect, that there is no such thing as a woman's honour, or if there is, it is only to be a bulwark against a weak temptation. When the temptation is strong enough, not only is the tempted person justified in yielding, but such yielding becomes not merely inevitable but something to be welcomed and glorified.

It is not for nothing that the world has learned to think of a woman's honour as involving a peculiar sacrifice. The general Voice of Mankind is right when, if it speaks of a woman's dishonour, it means thereby a sacrifice to her purity in mind and body.[21]

In other words, what rankles Strachey is Wells's refusal to accept the double standard. However, Wells's attack was not against that standard but against social mores which refused to allow women to act as human beings. There is nothing promiscuous about the virginal Ann who fell in love and showed it. In fact, in Wells's handling, the evil lies less with the woman than with the man.

Ann Veronica was smeared but not subjected to the direct suppression of Shaw's banned play of a decade earlier, *Mrs. Warren's Profession*. Read today, the novel presents a heroine too innocent and trusting to be believed; she has nothing of the brittle brilliance of Vivie Warren or of the lyrical flights into passion of Lady Chatterly, for whom Wells's Ann paved the way. If Ann is the best realized of any of Wells's non-comic women characters, this is not to say she comes alive with the vibrancy of a Kipps or a Polly. Her motives are too carefully analyzed, thought processes too exhaustively explained, for her to be an artistically rendered character. There is is never a moment in Ann Veronica's soliloquies nearly so poignant as the closing scene of *Kipps* when Artie and Ann Pornick decide what a "rum go" everything is, or the one in which Mr. Polly decides against suicide when the flames are licking up about him.

Ann Veronica, for all its thematic stiffness, is never quite drowned in doctrine. Wells tries to bring the girl to life. Defiant, Ann goes to a science school in London where she falls in love with a teacher, a man named Capes, who is separated from his wife. That Wells should have dedicated the novel to his wife Jane is not surprising in the light of its autobiographical overtones; Wells had met her in tutorial sessions at a time when his first marriage was failing. When Ann and Capes decide, after much wrestling with conscience, to elope, one has a variation on the situation between Isabel and Remington in *Machiavelli*. Wells was fond of exploiting similar domestic situations from book to book by switching the angle of interest from character to character.

Although unquestionably a tour-de-force novel in an age which still considered Ibsen's plays daring, *Ann Veronica* is a markedly unsatisfactory performance. Wells does not lead Ann to any startling answer to Victorian propriety. She has demanded the right to be free, but she settles for a conventional marriage. Her conventional relatives recognize that her rebellion is condoned by her ultimate submission. Ann's "woman's role" is still what the Victorians decreed: a biological one.[22]

Reading the novel today is such a task that the reader is hard-pressed to take St. Loe Strachey at his word when he describes the novel as "capable of poisoning the minds of those who read it."[23] Brome writes that the book took "an audacious step in the development of the modern English novel, bringing alive the contemporary circumstance of physical love, but it seems laughingly innocent when read today and needs no defence."[24] Although Wells demonstrates conclusively that "talk" in a novel can explain the idea of love between two people, he falls desperately short in portraying passion in its higher, intenser moods. Capes, who has eloped with Ann Veronica to Switzerland, speaks with unlyrical self-consciousness to his lover: " 'To think,' he cried, 'you are ten years younger than I! . . . there are times when you make me feel a little thing at your feet—a young, silly, protected thing. Do you know, Ann Veronica, it is all a lie about your birth certificate; a forgery—and fooling at that. You are one of the immortals. Immortal! You were in the beginning, and all the men in the world who have known what love is have worshipped at your feet . . . you are the High Priestess of Life' " (pp. 375–76).

III   Marriage (*1912*) *and Others*

That Ann Veronica and Capes were not to go on to a married life of unalloyed bliss is indicated in *Marriage,* the novel that tells the story of Ann Veronica's fortunes in matrimony. Marjorie Pope is substituted for Ann, and Trafford for Capes. Even the minor characters are projections of people in the earlier novel. Mr. Pope becomes Mr. Stanley—both fathers of the bride—and Magnet substitutes for Manning, each an unsuccessful suitor. Marjorie's and Trafford's life together is happy until Marjorie's inclination to social-climbing forces Trafford to abandon research for industry and finance. Trafford, a maturation of Wells's earliest persona—the creative man of science, a line beginning with Prendick in *Dr. Moreau*—is obliged to lay aside his researches in molecular physics to work out a successful process for synthetic rubber.

Trafford makes a fortune, but his affluence becomes stultifying; his life loses meaning; his marriage crumbles from within. Wells apparently, according to Edwin E. Slosson, had adopted a theory about the normal division of labor between husband and wife: the man should be an expert in the art of getting money and the woman in the art of handling it.[25] A kind of Thorstein Veblen dilemma intervenes: both Marjorie and Trafford regard their duties as ends in themselves; she, to buy things they neither want nor need; he, to be over-absorbed in business. The solution, however, is straight out of Thoreau. Their life is swamped, Wells contends, by restless activity, commercial strivings, and the loss of their identities. Their Walden is the wilds of Labrador. They live in a tent, and discuss marriage and life until Marjorie gains a new conception of the vocation of a wife. As Nicholson puts it: "She is to be a help-meet to the Wellsian cave-man, dreaming of his world state before the camp fire," [26] for one of the rules Wells proposed for the élite of his Modern Utopia was that a man who aspired to be a leader should for a week every year go off into the desert and live in solitude.

Trafford and Marjorie extend their utopian respite to a year. The story ends happily though inconclusively, for Wells does not solve woman's problem. Trafford aspires to an equivalent of George Ponderevo's unknowable "something," the collective force that rules life:

"It's something arising out of life—not the common stuff of life. An exhalation. . . . It's like the little tongues of fire that came at Pentecost. . . . Perhaps I shall die a Christian yet. . . . The other Christians won't like me if I do. . . . It's what I reach up to, what I desire shall pervade me, not what I am. . . . Salvation! . . .

This flame that arises out of life, that redeems life from purposeless triviality, *isn't* life. Let me get hold of that. . . . (p. 531)

The novel appears to be pointing to Wells's short-lived World War I phase when he so exasperated T. S. Eliot and a whole host of former disciples by contriving a series of substitute religions[27] and even, with the publication of *Mr. Britling,* "finding God."

In the two novels directly following *Marriage,* Wells plays on variations of the same theme of the search for a "true life of dialogue." In *The Wife of Sir Isaac Harman* (1914), Wells deals with a woman's fight for freedom against the tyranny, not of a father as in *Ann Veronica,* but of an elderly husband. In *The Passionate Friends* (1913), which combines elements of *Isaac Harman* and *The New Machiavelli,* Lady Harman and the estranged wife of Remington—the former in conversation and the latter in letters—both record the conviction that women have been trapped by their biological role, by their inability to resist easy relegation to the "doll's house." Only a basic change in the mutual attitudes of the two sexes will allow women to break free from biological bondage and to help free mankind from the tyranny of sex.

World War I and Wells's preoccupations with the elaborate pamphleteering for a world state which culminated in *The Outline of History* caused Wells to abandon the writing of novels dealing with the frustrations of marriage. However, in 1937, Wells wrote *Brynhild,* a study of a woman caught in the futile eddies of a marriage. Unable to find any satisfactory role to play, Brynhild turns finally to that of mother.

A year later, out of the wreckage of a rancorous liaison, Wells wrote *Apropos of Dolores.* The novel deals with a woman who spends herself in jealousy and vindictiveness when her desire for children has been thwarted. Whether the book was a *roman à clef,* a reply to a devastating attack by his one-time companion, is immaterial here.[28] The novel closes out a lengthy phase of his career devoted to what a recent study of Wells terms "the marriage-cycle novels." Dr. Doris Schwalbe concludes that the novels which began with *Love and Mr. Lewisham* and ended nearly forty years later with *Apropos of Dolores* are important because Wells "gives new insight into the causes for these frustrations [of both sexes]. He looks beyond the usual economic and social forces and sees biological differences as the primary activating force. Wells believes that men and women must regard one another as equal, but different. Men and women must learn to respect the creative potentialities of each sex." [29]

CHAPTER 8

The Novel of Ideas

I Of Art, Of Literature, Of Mr. Henry James

IF one were of a mind to defend Wells's modus operandi as a novelist, he could do no worse than to call on the author's own words. Few authors, as George Orwell has said, had less vanity. Wells always downgraded his stature as an artist and a thinker by some temporary jockeying for position—thus his ploy to put off Henry James about preferring to be called "journalist" rather than "artist," or that ironic subtitle of his autobiography, *Discoveries and Conclusions of a Very Ordinary Brain.* By seeming to undervalue his own works, by comparing them to the dirty scratchings made by a beetle once imprisoned by the young Bertie Wells, he helped to blind critics to the sheer literary brilliance of his earlier work.

Perhaps the most devastating single utterance against the Wellsian novel, one so brilliant that it never produced a reply, was Virginia Woolf's trenchant view through a Bloomsbury keyhole of the death of characterization in the Edwardians—Wells, Bennett, and Galsworthy.[1] However, to demolish Wells, as Mrs. Woolf sought to do, on the basis, undeniably valid, that individual characterization stood for less and less in his novels as he went on, would be to overlook how brilliantly the intimations of his novels, even some of the bad ones, dramatized the aspirations of the generation that was still young during World War I. "There was, conceivably, not much wisdom to be gained from [Wells]. But there was a great deal of exhilaration—the wine, of all wines, keenest on the palate of youth. And upon youth—not literary youth merely, but youth substantially and at large—no writer was to have a comparable influence until George Orwell. . . ."[2]

Stanley Kauffmann, in a moving eulogy to Wells's dying voice among young readers of the 1930's, declares that his influence declined sharply after 1925.[3] This estimate is probably a few years on the generous side since *Mr. Britling* (1916) was probably the last of his novels to sell in substantial numbers in the United States. Speaking as this book did for both the doomed soldier in the trenches and the grief-stricken parents, actual and potential, at home, it had a vogue few novels written during the heat of war could equal. *William Clissold* (1926) was Wells's last serious bid to right himself, but its tired frettings of an aging seer reached only the members of the generation that had grown old with him.

Curiously enough, it was as a historian that Wells's meteor soared for the last time. *The Outline of History* (1919–1920), whatever its reception from specialists, was an immensely popular success with sales in English of more than a half a million copies within three years of publication.[4] Its continued use as a standard book for homes assured the presence of the famous name within the average reader's horizon. But the concentrated effort required by the *Outline* caused a three-year rupture in novel writing which, by his own acknowledgment, Wells was never able to repair.[5] *The Undying Fire* (1919) was Wells's first and only successful experiment with a novel done wholly in dialogue; but it was also among his last well-received novels. *The Secret Places of the Heart,* published three years later, began a twenty-year languor which voluminous production, one or more a year until 1942, could not hide.

It is difficult to reconcile Wells's long sterility as a novelist with the critical acclaim he won early in his career. For fifteen years everything he touched turned to gold. First, there was the acknowledged originality and excellence of the five scientific romances described in Chapter Three. Alone, however, these could not win him stature as a novelist. They were a variation of the term Graham Greene uses to describe his own early works—"entertainments"—and recognition as a novelist was not accorded Wells until the publication of *Love and Mr. Lewisham* in 1900.

"Written with greater care than any of the . . . earlier books," [6] *Mr. Lewisham* never received the acclaim Wells had hoped for it. That would come five years later with the publication of *Kipps.* Nonetheless Henry James wrote Wells of finding in *Lewisham* "a great charm and a great deal of the real thing—that is of the note of life, if not *all* of it (as distinguished from the said great deal). . . . I am not quite sure that I see your *idea*—I mean your Subject, so to speak, as determined or constituted. . . ." [7]

The "determined or constituted" fabric of the novel—its adherence to the canons of the form—would forge within a few years an irreparable breach between James and his younger contemporary.

Leon Edel and Gordon N. Ray trace the meeting of James and Wells back to 1898 although, as a young drama critic on *Pall Mall,* Wells had been present three years before when James was humiliated by an audience which booed when he appeared on the stage at the opening of his play *Guy Domville.* Their ages aside— James, fifty-five; Wells, thirty-two—no more curious literary pairing could be imagined:

> The paradox of [James's] life was that, although unread, he remained a literary lion. His opinions on the art of fiction were valued; he was *cher maître* to Joseph Conrad. . . . He was established as a great American man of letters who had chosen England as his home. . . .

> Wells, on the other hand, was still a struggling writer. . . . By origin he belonged . . . "below stairs," but his sharp intelligence and formidable energy, conveyed to the public by a nimble pen, were allowing him to wander about increasingly in the drawing-room.[8]

Edwardian England was a time when "deans" like James made it a point to welcome young writers like Wells into the fold. Dorothy Richardson and Frank Swinnerton have portrayed best the atmosphere at Spade House, Sandgate, where in 1900 H. G. and Jane Wells made their new home a central point for artists of all descriptions—those established, about to be, or never to be. Miss Richardson, especially, in her series of novels collectively titled *Pilgrimage,* conveys the rampant unsureness with which Wells, who acknowledged himself to be Hypo Wilson in her novel, strove for recognition in a literary society which Henry James ruled by a kind of age-before-glamor noblesse.[9]

From almost the start, James welcomed Wells as, for him, by far the most interesting novelist of his generation—"in fact, the only interesting one." [10] Sandgate lay across Romney Marsh from James's bachelor quarters in Rye, and the two began to meet often. Wells, shortly before he rushed to Provence to be at Gissing's deathbed, brought the ill-fated Gissing to visit James. James and Wells were frequently joined by Conrad, or Arnold Bennett, or by Stephen Crane who had "borrowed" Brede House near Rye during the last year of his short life.

A James biographer, Michael Swan, may be extravagant when he suggests that the James-Wells relationship was that of father and son; but the statement makes much sense when Swan, in his perplexity over why James should have become so excited over a writer so unlike himself, asks: "Was he [James] simply recognizing genius in whatever form it should appear—or was this recognition inspired by some obscure demand of his private psychology? Did he admire Wells as the aesthete secretly admires the athlete? Wells's commonsense pragmatism attracts him in the same way that he was unwillingly drawn towards the mind of his brother William. . . ." [11] Whether James's solicitude for Wells stemmed from a total dedication to craft or from a psychic need does not concern us here. It is enough to note that the master bestowed his favors lavishly on the pupil, and the pupil received them with the deference of the aspiring pretender. Yet, as their relationship lengthened and as Wells's burgeoning fame buttressed his Cockney impudence, an implication of disapproval crept into James's letters.

After James's unalloyed praise of *Kipps* ("It left me prostrate with admiration . . . a mere born gem . . . of such a brilliancy of *true* truth. . . . You have for the very first time treated the English 'lower middle' class, etc., without the picturesque, the grotesque, the fantastic and romantic interference [of] Dickens . . . [and] George Eliot"),[12] James became more reserved about *Ann Veronica;* he found the main characterization wanting in "clearness and *nuances*." [13] Although praising the first half of *The New Machiavelli,* James excoriated Wells for the first time on "that accursed autobiographic form which puts a premium on the loose, the improvised, the cheap and easy." [14] His view of *Marriage* was almost explicitly dark: ". . . I find myself absolutely unable, and still more unwilling, to approach you, or to take leave of you, in any projected light of criticism, in any judging or concluding, any comparing, in fact in any aesthetic or 'literary,' relation at all; and this in spite of the fact that the light of criticism is almost that in which I most fondly bask. . . ." [15]

The outlines of H. G. Wells's thorough abdication from the art of the novel become clear to anyone reading his correspondence with Henry James. James deplored long narratives in the first person because they precipitated the novel into "looseness. . . . The terrible *fluidity* of self-revelation." Two of Wells's best novels, *Tono-Bungay* and *The New Machiavelli,* are written in first person and have long monologues. James objected to having characters "talk at" the reader rather than revealing themselves through unconscious behavior or telling incident. *Ann Veronica* and *Marriage,* though written in third person, are often painfully essayistic; the explicit ideas are on display rather than insightful behavior. James excused Wells, at least on the surface, for his transgressions on the basis of the younger man's matchless vitality —James always called it, without disparagement, "cheek"—and could write to Mrs. Humphrey Ward: ". . . I really think him [Wells] more interesting by his faults than he will probably ever manage to be in any other way; and he is a most vivid and violent object lesson!" [16]

Wells answered the criticism of mandarin critics like Henry James in the only way that he knew. All his writing life Wells had flayed Victorian obsolescence by calling for a revolution against debilitating social and political strictures. He now resorted to equivalent action in the pursuance of his craft. If his novels were deficient in the qualities Henry James said were *sine qua nons*— and Wells, rather than denying it, said such canons omitted the facts that novels could be something else, too—then Wells would simply call for anarchy. His pleas were first made in the essay "The Scope of the Novel," published in *Fortnightly Review* (November, 1911) and *Atlantic Monthly* (January, 1912). They were repeated twenty years later in his autobiography in the chapter "Digression about Novels," and stated again near the end of his career in the foreword to *Babes in the Darkling Wood* (1940).

Wells, in effect, sought to stretch the novel to cover almost anything that could be made interesting in the form of fiction. Behind the culminating argument put forth in the quotation below, one can hardly miss the urgency in the voice of a newly established fictionist who, in 1911, was aware as a professional writer that in Edwardian England it was extremely difficult to publish and get people to read anything unless it could be classified as a novel and go on the six-shilling shelf, subject to a discount of one and sixpence:[17]

And this being my view you will be prepared for the demand I am now about to make for an absolutely free hand for the novelist in his choice of topic and incident and in his method of treatment. . . . We are going to write, subject only to our limitations, about the whole of human life. We are going to deal with political questions and religious questions and social questions. We cannot present people unless we have this free hand, this unrestricted field. . . . We mean to deal with these things, and it will need very much more than the disapproval of provincial librarians, the hostility of a few influential people in London . . . to stop the incoming tide of aggressive novel-writing. We are going to write about it all. . . . Before we have done, we will have all life within the scope of the novel.[18]

In 1914, Henry James wrote what was, in a sense, an answer to Wells's proclamation for *The Times Literary Supplement* in a two-installment article, "The Younger Generation," which he expanded for inclusion in *Notes on Novelists,* published the same year. Edel and Ray find this attempt to assess both the middle generation of writers—Conrad, Bennett, Galsworthy, and Wells— and the younger—Hugh Walpole, Gilbert Cannan, Compton Mackenzie, and a thirtyish newcomer from the Midlands named D. H. Lawrence—"in some ways his least responsible piece of criticism." [19] The essay, patronizing throughout, fails in its courtesy and syntactical deviousness to hide James's contempt for the kind of novels Wells and Bennett were writing:

We confound the author of *Tono-Bungay* and the author of *Clayhanger* in this imputation for the simple reason that with the sharpest differences of character and range they yet come together under our so convenient measure of value by *saturation.* This is the greatest value, to our sense, in either of them, their other values, even when at the highest, not being quite in proportion to it; and as to be saturated is to be documented, to be able even on occasion to prove quite enviably and potently so, they are alike in the authority that creates emulation.[20]

James damns with faint praise Well's penchant for "absorbing knowledge at the pores" and Bennett's "density of illustration." In other words, in Wells and Bennett, Henry James saw the defects of the virtue of saturation. It left out the need for what James called a "centre of interest or . . . sense of the whole."

James then attacks in earnest when he refers to novels like *Kipps, Tono-Bungay,* and *Ann Veronica*—works he had lavishly praised in correspondence—as blunting critical judgment by their "blinding, bluffing vivacity." For *Marriage,* he reserves, however, his major onslaught: ". . . we wince at a certain quite peculiarly gratuitous sacrifice to the casual in *Marriage* very much as at see-ing some fine and indispensable little part of a mechanism slip through *profane fingers* and lose itself." [21]

The novel's "gratuitous sacrifice to the casual" was the open declaration of love between two strangers—Marjorie and Trafford —after a three-hour interlude, noted but not described in the book. The "profane fingers," though descriptive of an analogy James had drawn, could not help but have angered Wells who was sensitive to the fact that Mrs. Ward was not the only one of the mandarins who regarded him as coarse and that his reputation as something of a rake who openly cohabited with maidens with-out benefit of clergy might have influenced James's estimate of him as an artist.

Later, in the autobiography, Wells elaborately defended his dis-inclination to provide psychological preparation for a love affair that flowered on such short notice. But, in 1914, the score with James could not be settled by one of their long talks in James's garden at Rye. For his retaliatory thrust, Wells dusted off an old manuscript he had conceived as early as 1901 and had returned to periodically during his years of infamy in the wake of *Ann Veron-ica.* In 1914 he somewhat recast the book *Boon,* appended a chapter entitled "Of Art, Of Literature, Of Mr. Henry James,"—a chaotic though frequently perceptive satire of the Jamesian novel and a cruel caricature of the man behind it.

Boon was a book Wells came to regret. There is only one refer-ence to it in his autobiography. It was a wrongheaded effort, but an understandable one in the total picture of Wells. Under a cer-tain surface comedy, it is the cup-runneth-over indignation of an outsider lashing out at the literary establishment. It gave violent answer to the brahmins of London society who always considered him hopelessly "below stairs"; to the Fabians and their "Episode of Mr. Wells"; to the "Reform Club Myth" that impugned him morally, socially, and intellectually. It followed by three years his attack on the Webbs in *The New Machiavelli.* Such angry-young-man works would have their equivalents in angry-middle-aged-man and angry-old-man effusions for the next thirty years.

The *Boon* aftermath is too well known to be sketched in detail here. Wells left a copy for James at his club, a gesture Edel and Ray deplore but one which Wells had followed since the publication of *Kipps* a decade earlier. James's letter of acknowledgment and the one following Wells's apology terminated their friendship and established—supremely—the Jamesian esthetic:

I *have* no view of life and literature, I maintain, other than that our form of the latter in especial is admirable exactly by its range and variety, its plasticity and liberality, its fairly living on the sincere and shifting experience of the individual practitioner. That is why I have always so admired your so free and strong application of it, the particular rich receptacle of intelligences and impressions emptied out with an energy of its own, that your genius constitutes; and *that* is in particular why, in my letter of two or three days since, I pronounced it curious and interesting that you should find the case I constitute myself only ridiculous and vacuous to the extent of your having to proclaim your sense of it. . . .[22]

And, finally, James wrote: "It is art that *makes* life, makes interest, makes importance, for our consideration and application of these things, and I know of no substitute whatever for the force and beauty of its process. . . ."[23]

Without question, James, perplexed and troubled by the neglect of his books, had triumphed over the more popular, the better-rewarded Wells. The following fragments from a letter written by Wells to James, dated three days after James's art-makes-life epistle, show all too well how easily Wells's outsider's unsureness —his short view of life and art—had cast him irrevocably into the position of the Philistine clutching, like a life-raft, anti-poetic utilitarianism: "I don't clearly understand your concluding phrases— which shews no doubt how completely they define our difference. When you say 'it is art that *makes* life, makes interest, makes importance,' I can only read sense into it by assuming that you are using 'art' for every conscious human activity. I use the word for a research and attainment that is technical and special."[24]

There is an interesting parallel to the James-Wells correspondence in an exchange of letters between Wells and James Joyce in

1928. At Wells's request, Joyce, hopeful of receiving the assistance of the then-influential Wells in the publicizing of his novel, had sent him some installments of *Ulysses*. The Wells who had trumpeted for absolute freedom of subject matter in 1911 now, seventeen years later, called Joyce's work "a considerable thing. . . . But I don't think it gets anywhere." He discounted Joyce's masterwork as an "extraordinary experiment" which he would help save from the censors but one that for him "is a dead end." [25] Wells was as little able to see anything beyond his uses for art in 1928 as James was able to see beyond *ars pro arte* in 1915. Time vindicated Joyce over Wells, but it has not vindicated Wells over James.

Wells closed a final letter of apology to James with an admission which, whether made to assuage James or to dam up the flood of adverse criticism his increasingly hybrid novels were receiving, can be taken to mark a cleft between what was and what was to be. "I had rather," Wells asserts, "be called a journalist than an artist. . . ." [26] Wells had reached the definitive breaking-off point from the intuitive, fresh way of looking at the human condition—the stance that had brought off the handful of books for which he will be remembered.

More than any other single factor, the coming of World War I solved for Wells his problems of art-versus-doctrine. The first shell exploded Wells into an arena of combat far different from the literary game of the Edwardians whose rules he had already begun to violate. Though *Boon* was the work of an irritated participant, its reception—an avalanche of disapproval—showed that Wells, like Remington, had not yet earned, perhaps never could earn, the right to flaunt those rules. With the outbreak of war, H. G. Wells assumed a new public persona. He became a kind of *insider*, the image of the reasoning Englishman counseling a liberal interpretation of war. He placed himself firmly on record as pro-Ally, anti-German; and the title of one of his pamphlets, *The War That Will End War*, became an international slogan. The angry young man had become, at fifty, the spokesman for all who sought assurance amidst the whirlwind of disaster.

II Mr. Britling Sees It Through (*1916*)

"If posterity wants to know what England felt during the first two years of the Great War," wrote Sidney Dark, ". . . there is no contemporary record . . . that will tell it so much [as *Mr. Britling*]." [27] Wells, ever a writer in a hurry, declined to wait for the war to end to reflect on it in tranquility. He made a novel out of the war—not out of one campaign, not out of one soldier's adventures, but out of the war as a whole. Wells took for his central figure one Britling, an essayist and philosopher of advanced tendencies. In describing Britling's reactions to the war, Wells traced their development from the first angry amazement to the final extraordinary readjustment of theories and hopes.

The work is best classed as higher journalism, a term not intended to devalue it. Wells spreads a fictional veneer over topical main structure. Much of the novel is documentary, filled with actual names of living personages and with debates on current issues by intellectuals of the stripe Wells might be expected to lead —simple but sophisticated humanitarians who are disillusioned as to the value of cults and labels and who are emancipated, enlightened, cynical, but doggedly progressive. *Mr. Britling* reads in places like a book of current history. References to living personalities—Lloyd George, the Kaiser, Winston Churchill, Shaw—and the transparent disguises of the well-known military and political figures all contribute to the documentary characteristic of the book.

Wells frequently interrupts the flow of narrative to present a vivid communique on a historical event. This news-flash announces the shootings at Sarajevo, the prelude to war: "And indeed at the very moment when Mr. Britling was saying these words, in Sarajevo in Bosnia, where the hour was somewhat later, men whispered together, and one held nervously to a black parcel that had been given him and nodded as they repeated his instructions, a black parcel with certain unstable chemicals and a curious arrangement of detonators therein, a black parcel destined ultimately to shatter nearly every landmark of Mr. Britling's cosmogony . . ." (pp. 59–60). The novel reads as if Wells, while keeping before the reader Britling's fictional life, also spreads out the newspaper Britling is reading. The placing of Britling's life

[106]

against a backdrop of historical events leading inexorably to World War I gives the book great value as a record.

Britling, however, is clearly the work of a novelist rather than a reporter. No journal of events can legitimately pose as fiction without verisimilitude of setting and characters. Mr. Britling, as was customary for a writer who never drew his heroes from other than his own stock, is H. G. Wells; and the setting is Wells's own household during the first year of the war. Sidney Dark shows how Matching's Easy of the novel is little altered from Wells's Essex country house, Easton Glebe; and he identifies the gallery of personages in the novel by name, but the reactions, so exhaustively developed, are those of the English in general.

The spirit of the novel is the gradual forming of disillusionment as the cruel facts of war close in on civilized men who will not, until almost too late, believe in them. Wells shows his kinship to the journalist by his "arrangement" of characters. He employs an American, Mr. Direck, secretary of the Massachusetts Society for the Study of Contemporary Thought, to report an outsider's impressions of an unenterprising, sluggish, prosperous, and comfortable England on the brink of disaster. Direck is literally a reporter, and the impressions gathered through the eyes that Wells gives him tend to materialize into correspondent's dispatches.

Wells adds to his carefully-planned gallery of representative figures that of Herr Heinrich, who lives with the Britlings as a tutor. The interviews with Heinrich contrast the German psyche—its definiteness and its order—with England's tendency to muddle through and America's youthful self-reliance. Sidney Dark observes the thoroughness of Wells's understanding of the American point of view, the reasons why she hesitated long before entering the war.

The novel has hardly begun when, through the eyes of Direck, one is placed in the center of a Wellsian symposium. Wells chooses for his opinion forum a representative group. Britling (Wells) is the advance-guard Republican with "ideas in the utmost profusion about races and empires and social order and political institutions and gardens and automobiles and the future of India and China and aesthetics and America and the education of mankind in general . . ." (p. 12). His antagonist in the opening dialogues is Lady Frensham, aristocratic and resistant to change, who is made to represent the body of upper-class English minds that can see no danger of the Empire's breaking down and that are violent only in their opposition to minor skirmishes waged by the suffragettes or by the advocates of Irish Home Rule. A third participant is Lady Homartyn who represents the complacent social woman in passive resistance to post-Victorian social forces. Wells portrays her as "incapable of believing that she won't always be able to have week-ends at Claverings, and that the letters and the tea won't come to her bedside in the morning" (p. 434).

Wells craftily introduces the events leading up to war—and some of his hindsight bulletins have an interpretive brilliance only possible in a super-journalist of wide intellectual grasp who is able to look at Present from viewpoints of Past and Future. Britling, for all his prescience, delivers ironic commentaries on the impossibility of catastrophe. When the war does come, he records and analyzes the growing hardness of heart and the scarring over of British conscience that was destined to be re-enacted, when Wells was in his late seventies, in World War II.

Wells was fifty when he wrote *Mr. Britling*, but even into middle age Wells wrote with an eye on the young. Hugh Britling, son of the title character, becomes Wells's *deus ex machina* for his formulation, at the end of the novel, of a faith in God. But throughout the early part of the novel Hugh is merely a part of the Wellsian symposium, a chip off the old block. Hugh's analysis of a Britain mired in tradition is full of Wellsian irony: "'. . . In England everybody talks of change and nothing ever changes. Nothing changes in England, because the people who want to change things change their minds before they change anything else. I've been to London talking for the last half-year. Studying art they call it. Before that I was a science student, and I want to be one again. Don't you think . . . there's something about science—it's steadier than anything else in the world?'" (pp. 66-67). And, later, to Direck, the American reporter, Hugh says: "'Dad says in one of his books that over here we are being and over there [in America] you are beginning. It must be tremendously stimulating to think that your country is still being made. . . . Unless something tumbles down here, we never think of altering it and even then we just shore it up'" (p. 67). The autobiographical tendency is unmistakable, for what Hugh Britling says reflects Wells's faith in the infinite plasticity of the United States. Two decades later he spoke of President Franklin D. Roosevelt and Stalin as the world's most important figures—as men concerned with becoming rather than being.

Events move rapidly to a tragic conclusion. Hugh goes to France; his letters from the trenches form much of the book. Herr Heinrich is called back to Germany for conscription, and his sentimental farewell to his English friends is one of the best things in the book. With Britling as commentator, the story moves steadily to its climax. When the fatal telegram bears the news that Hugh has been killed, Britling takes his loss in a strange spirit. He declares that he is neither angry nor depressed, only "bitterly hurt" by the end of something fine. For Wells, it is not enough to present a grieving Mr. Britling. Wells is obsessed by the human folly. However, a Wells without a solution is inconceivable. The one he offers had been strongly hinted at four years earlier in *Marriage* when Trafford referred to life as being redeemed by the flame of salvation. In *Britling*, Wells presents an embellishment. In his bitter sorrow, Mr. B.—H. G. Wells—finds God. But his God is not an omnipotent God. He is not responsible for the horrors of human life, but someday He will triumph and then horror will cease. Cruelty, injustice, and aggression are present in the world; but so also are kindness, goodness, love, and these qualities are the signs of God—the God who struggles, the God who will ultimately prevail. To a mind like Wells's—rationalistic and suspicious of spiritual values—any lengthy phase in passionate embrace of the idea that the meek will inherit the earth was hardly to be expected.

Nevertheless, in its time, *Mr. Britling* became a household word on two continents. Mr. Britling's loss mirrored other losses of loved ones from the British Midlands to the American plains. The novel was a *succès d'estime*—Wells said it earned him twenty thousand pounds in the United States alone. Because men and women growing to maturity in the first twenty years of the new century looked to H. G. Wells for a path out of the woods, the picture of a Wells-with-a-deity was a compelling one. Years later, Wells, whose own sons were too young to serve in the war of

1914–18, wrote that enthusiastic strangers often invaded his home with the demand to see the place where he had wept when he had heard of his son's death in battle.

III   *Sunset of Divinity:*
The Undying Fire (*1919*) *and Others*

The H. G. Wells whom Chesterton found too much in a state of reaction could not long accept the conversion of his New Republic into a divine monarchy. His "theocratic phase" lasted exactly four years and four books. From God, the Captain of the World Republic, as discovered by Wells through Mr. Britling, Wells proceeded in *God the Invisible King* (1917) to a thoroughly nondoctrinal, almost metaphoric deity who is in the nature of an "inspiring but extremely preoccupied comrade, a thoroughly hard leader." The same year, with *The Soul of a Bishop,* he distinguished between the God of the formal religionists and the Wellsian God, who was the personification of human progressiveness, an embodiment of the collective mind of race which Wells had placed on view in *First and Last Things* and *Tono-Bungay.* Norman Nicholson comments that the Bishop is the nearest Wellsian equivalent to a prig.[28]

Wells was candid about this interlude—a period which T. S. Eliot may have had in mind when he called Wells's "a substitute religion"[29]: "I cannot disentangle . . . what was simple and direct in this theocratic phase in my life, from what was—*politic.* I do not know how far I was being perfectly straightforward . . . how far I was . . . 'coddling myself,' and how far I was trying to make my New Republicanism acceptable in a different guise to that multitude which could not, it seemed, dispense with kingship."[30] It would almost be possible to dismiss the god-fearing interlude as one induced by Wells's growing penchant for watering down his message to that form which would reach the largest popular audience. However, in 1919, he wrote *The Undying Fire,* a modern adaptation of the Book of Job. Wells regarded it as the best of those novels which he modelled on the Platonic Dialogue and which occupied him to the end of his life; and Vincent Brome, writing in 1951, called it a noble and profound religious work "obscured by lesser books."[31]

In the novel, Job Huss (Job of Uz), borne down by pain and

trouble, is staying at a dingy retreat. Until lately he has been successful in a Wellsian way as head of a school—Woldingstanton—where he works diligently to evolve a curriculum based on the study of man's place in the historical and evolutionary process. Misfortune has struck, like Job's boils, from all sides. Two boys die at the school during an epidemic, and two more are burned to death in a school fire; an assistant master is killed in a lab explosion; Huss's savings are lost by his solicitor's speculations; and he and his wife receive the news of their only son's death in France. Huss's physical pain is diagnosed as cancer; an immediate operation is advised. On the morning of the operation Huss is visited by two governors of the school and by Farr, the man who is to take his place. The greater part of the novel is a record of the conversation between Huss and his visitors. Knowing that the operation may be fatal, Huss speaks to them as sincerely as possible.

Huss discusses the task of the teacher, reviews his lifework, and shows how it would all be nullified if Farr were appointed. The men talk about religion, theology, the beauty and cruelty of Nature (there is a magnificent evocation of T. H. Huxley's old fear that civilization—man—might fail to turn back the forces of nature), and the apparent indifference to God. Huss's physician contributes the agnostic view that the Godly Process is beyond man's comprehension. Huss tells them that, in spite of their varying ideas, the four of them are alike in that they submit to things as they are. He alone does not submit; he rebels instead with the spirit within him. God, not all-powerful, struggles through Man to attain the organized unity of the world so that—competition, hatred, rivalry thrown aside—the race may sweep forward to ever new triumphs.

Then comes the operation; and, while Job is under chloroform, he becomes the Biblical Job who talks with God and, unlike the Old Testament version, with Satan, too. Courage burns like an undying fire within man, God tells Job; and, so long as that fire does not go out, there are no limits to man's achievements. At the close of their dialogue, God also tells Job of the fearful alternative: ". . . If that courage fail, if that sacred fire go out, then all things fail and all things go out, all things—good and evil, space and time" (p. 160).

The Undying Fire is the last of Wells's middle-period books, fictional counterparts of *The Outline of History* which promised a Wellsian grail. Rebecca West, reviewing *The Research Magnificent* in 1915, found in the Great Promise of that work and in all the Wells novels of the period "a temple for our homeless faiths, a place of beauty where we can satisfy the human instinct for high endeavors, a place of power where we can compromise our ambition, the leadership of the world." [32] J. Middleton Murry, looking back to the period of his youth, said of Wells: "He was our standard bearer and fought for us so bravely that when he failed we failed with him." [33]

In *The Research Magnificent*, Benham, the researcher after true aristocracy, stands in the moonlight of the Bengal jungle, facing a tiger and lifting a lean hand to it: "I am Man," he intones; and the beast "vanished, became invisible and inaudible with a kind of instantaneousness" (p. 48). For Edmund Wilson, the zeal of his youth lighted by the effulgence of all Wells's books written during the two golden decades of 1895–1915, the reading of that scene brought an abrupt falling-out.[34] "Once, he had given us to breathe an air of exalting hope; now, he was numbing us with bewilderment," wrote Odette Keun, another of Wilson's generation.[35] But the books that adhered to an airy philosophy which seemed to conclude that, if only men wait long enough, all will be well, became inadequate and bewildering to even Wells's staunchest disciples. Thirty books, each contradicting the previous one and all assuming whistling-in-the-dark postures that sought to exalt a world being enveloped by the shadow of totalitarianism, could neither redeem the world nor its once-influential spokesman. Indeed, the vast edifice of idea-novels H. G. Wells had begun constructing after *Tono-Bungay* was crumbling from within. The shift from novels well within the Edwardian tradition to novels of ideas whose heroes "were self-conscious pioneers in world rebuilding" cost Wells the serious attention of perceptive readers who expected first-rank fiction from him. The man whom the *New York Times*, at his death, called "the greatest public teacher of our time," [36] had lost his influential private audience—the intellectual caste represented by men like Edmund Wilson, Aldous Huxley, and George Orwell.

CHAPTER 9

World State

I *Brave New Worlder:* When The Sleeper Awakes (*1899*)

ANTHONY West has observed that one of the difficulties of
writing about Wells is that his mind was an undisciplined
mechanism which apparently contradicted in one book what it
had concluded in another. One can well imagine the perplexity of
the disciple in H. G. Wells's heyday trying to reconcile all those
New Republics, Open Conspiracies, Collective Minds of Race,
Universal Citizenrys, World Theocracies. While Wells's lifelong
strivings to close a gap left by the previous book—somehow to
make right in the next book the folly of those "moments of leaping
ignorance" of the last—brought forth too many books too quickly,
it is easy to glean the one abiding passion of H. G. Wells's life: the
Future.

Wells suggests in his autobiography that his contact with Huxley and evolutionary speculation at his most receptive age went
far to produce this dominant preoccupation. Certainly such early
and tentative creations as *The Man of the Year Million,* first written in 1887, and *The Chronic Argonauts* (1888) led to *The Time
Machine* (1895). By the time the new century dawned Wells was
obsessed by the chances of a writer—drenched in the study of
both the physical sciences and social philosophy—to take a page
from William Morris and Edward Bellamy: to isolate the conflicts, trends, and threats intrinsic to the late nineteenth century;
and to project them into an accurate shape of things to come.

His earliest views of the future were dark. Had Wells suc-
cumbed to any of the serious illnesses that beset him before 1900
and written only *The Time Machine, The Island of Dr. Moreau,
The Invisible Man, The War of the Worlds,* and, especially, *When
the Sleeper Wakes* and "A Story of Days to Come," he and not
Aldous Huxley or Eugene Zamiatin would have been accorded the
distinction of being the father of the inverted utopia, the first of

the major dystopians.[1] Ostrog, the head of the super-corporation's governing body in *The Sleeper,* is, as Anthony West notes, the Wellsian equivalent of George Orwell's Big Brother.[2] The sleeper, a kind of utopian Rip Van Winkle, awakens four generations after he has inexplicably fallen asleep. He finds himself a master-capitalist, owner of half the world, a world where capital and labor—the symbolic Eloi and the Morlocks of *The Time Machine*—have irrevocably destroyed all possibilities of a constructively planned society. The sleeper, Graham, and the dictator, Ostrog, carry on innumerable colloquies about how his mindless capital came to rule the world and reduce men to automatons:

"In the old days [said Graham] we dreamt of a wonderful democratic life, of a time when all men would be equal and happy."

Ostrog looked at him steadfastly. "The day of democracy is past. . . . That day . . . ended when marching infantry, when common men in masses ceased to win the battles of the world, when costly cannon, great ironclads, and strategic railways became the means of power. To-day is the day of wealth. Wealth now is power as it never was power before—it commands earth and sea and sky. All power is for those who can handle wealth. . . ."

Graham did not answer immediately. He stood lost in sombre preoccupations.

"No," said Ostrog. "The day of the common man is past. On the open countryside one man is as good as another. . . . The earlier aristocracy had a precarious tenure of strength and audacity. . . . There were insurrections, duels, riots. The first real aristocracy, the first permanent aristocracy, came in with castles and armour, and vanished before the musket and bow. But this is the second aristocracy. The real one. Those days of gunpowder and democracy were only an eddy in the stream. The common man now is a helpless unit. In these days we have this great machine of the city, and an organization complex beyond his understanding." (pp. 393–94)

I quote at length from this early work because it is very likely the first novel of any literary merit to question the present-day concept of "progress." The Machine, as Wells feared in 1899, exploits human inertia and weakness. It parrots Boss Ostrog's every whim. Children of the laboring class are converted from any inclination to non-conformity into trustworthy machine-minders. A Pleasure City is set aside for Graham, but the rank and file have sallow faces and dull eyes and wear the pale blue canvas uniforms of the Labor Department.

Considering its date of publication, the book must be considered remarkable on another count. It contains a somewhat halting but nonetheless accurate description of aerial warfare fifteen years before World War I; four years before the Wright brothers made their first successful Kitty Hawk flight in 1903; and nine years before Bleriot flew across the Channel. Wells was later to make extended use of what was then called aeronautics in *Tono-Bungay* and to depict a full-scale aerial battle in *The War in the Air,* both extremely avant-garde subjects for 1908, let alone 1899. For other inventions, Wells draws on Edward Bellamy's *Looking Backward:* enormous automatic restaurants that have replaced dining rooms, modern methods of heating and lighting, television to enable people to witness the news, and the replacement of reading and writing by mechanical devices.[3]

Writing at the time of Wells's death in 1946, George Orwell, when his mind may have been dogged by the fears that would culminate in *1984,* was unstinting in his praise for the novel: "In [*The Sleeper Awakens*] . . . Wells drops all traces of optimism and forecasts a highly organized totalitarian society based quite frankly upon slave labor. In some ways it comes extremely close to what is actually happening [1946], or appears to be happening, in the modern world, and it is in any case an astonishing feat of detailed imaginative construction [and] . . . the extent to which it anticipates Aldous Huxley's *Brave New World* and other pessimistic Utopia books has not been generally recognized." [4]

Orwell's tribute is not without irony, for the anti-utopians generally and Aldous Huxley particularly have erected grave-markers over the spiritual *locus* where Wells's mid-career wishful thinking took him: the World State. Shortly before his death Huxley told a *Paris Review* interviewer that *Brave New World* was begun as a satire of Wells's *Men Like Gods* (1923).[5] As Professor Wagar points out, Wells frequently appears in fictional guise among twentieth-century counter-utopographers. No reader of Wells, for example, can read the early pages of C. S. Lewis's *Out of the Silent Planet* without recognizing that writer's respectful chiding of Wells and his apostasy. As E. F. Bleiler reminds, it must not be forgotten that Wells was spiritual godfather to the Huxleys, Orwells, Zamiatins—to the E. M. Forster who wrote "The Machine Stops." "Wells heard the voice in the wilderness before they, and wrote its message before they, sometimes in the same symbols." [6]

II Anticipations (*1901*) *and* A Modern Utopia (*1905*)

Wells has described *Anticipations* as the main arch of his work, the reasonable expectations he drew from an exceptionally rich creative imagination. *A Modern Utopia* is more speculative: a presentation, not so much of expectations, as of desires. The two books represent a change of stance from trepidation to confidence, and set forth in general that body of ideas which can be called Wellsian. In *Anticipations,* Wells extols the virtues of functional men—men, like himself, trained in science—and calls them "New Republicans." They will be managerial and technical people; no effete talkers will be allowed. Only this scientist élite will be equipped to build from the destruction of the old order a technologically organized world society.

Enry Straker is an embryo creation by George Bernard Shaw who, in *Man and Superman,* written the year *Anticipations* was published, saw with his piercing wit the flaw of depending on the emergence of an élite to rule the world scientifically. In the play, Tanner, the kind of jabberer-intellectual Wells's New Republicans would oust, baits Straker unmercifully for his pride in dropping his "aitches" and for his bourgeois attitudes moored to a fetish for efficiency:

TANNER: . . . But this chap [Straker] has been educated. Whats more, he knows that we havnt. What was that Board School of yours, Straker?

STRAKER: Sherbrooke Road.

TANNER: . . . Sherbrooke Road is a place where boys learn something: Eton is a boy farm where we are sent because we are nuisances at home, and because in after life, whenever a Duke is mentioned, we can claim him as an old school-fellow.

STRAKER: You dont know nothing about it, Mr. Tanner. It's not the Board School that does it: it's the Polytechnic.

TANNER: His university, Octavius. Not Oxford, Cambridge, Durham, Dublin, or Glasgow. . . . No, Tavy. Regent Street! Chelsea! the

Borough!—I dont know half their confounded names: these are
his universities, not mere shops for selling class limitations like
ours. You despise Oxford, Enry, dont you?

STRAKER: No, I dont. Very nice sort of place, Oxford, I should think,
for people that like that sort of place. They teach you to be a gentleman there. In the Polytechnic they teach you to be an engineer
or such like. See?

TANNER: Sarcasm, Tavy, sarcasm! Oh, if you could only see into
Enry's soul, the depth of his contempt for a gentleman, the ar-
rogance of his pride in being an engineer, would appall you. He
positively likes the car to break down because it brings out my
gentlemanly helplessness and his workman-like skill and resource.

STRAKER: Never you mind him, Mr. Robinson. He likes to talk. We
know him, dont we?

OCTAVIUS (earnestly): But theres a great truth at the bottom of what
he says. I believe most intensely in the dignity of labor.

STRAKER (unimpressed): Thats because you never done any, Mr.
Robinson. My business is to do away with labor. Youll get more
out of me and a machine than you will out of twenty laborers. . . .

TANNER: For Heaven's sake, Tavy, dont start him on political econ-
omy. He knows all about it; and we dont. Youre a poetic Socialist,
Tavy: he's a scientific one.[7]

This long Shavian passage, with its idiosyncratic Shavian punctu-
ation, is introduced for several reasons. The writing of *Anticipations* corresponded approximately to Wells's coming under the
wing of the Fabians. The passage shows certain objections to
Wells's efficient-engineer New Republican from Shaw, a representative Fabian and a man with no illusions about the adaptability
of the Enry Strakers to a new world order. Sidney and Beatrice
Webb criticized *Anticipations* because of Wells's failure to recognize the need and probability of a specialized governing class.
Like them, Shaw saw the insufficiency of the managerial-technical
breed to head the new republic.

Perhaps there is more wisdom in Wells's old friend Frank Swinnerton than in either Shaw or the Webbs. To Swinnerton, there
would be no room for Wells and his natural affection for individuals in any of his utopias stemming from *Anticipations* because
"he would either be put to death by the mandarins for being in-
tractable or would clamor for the restoration of our imperfect,
greedy, acquisitive, and amusing society, in which a man could

breathe without first obtaining a license to do so. It is no wonder that he loathes bureaucrats and drill-sergeants; his true passion is for liberty." [8] Or, as Max Beerbohm put it: "So this is Utopia, is it? Well/ I beg your pardon, I thought it was Hell." [9]

It is idle conjecture to weigh the possibilities for merger of the essentially anarchic spirit of the man Wells was with the scientific New Republicanism he visioned in *Anticipations* and presumably saw exemplified in himself. The bent for sociology, which St. John Ervine said was his ruination, and for prophecy, which claimed him a new audience, could no longer be denied. *Mankind in the Making* (1903) stressed educational reform in a movement to bring Wells's New Republic to England and America. *The Food of the Gods* (1904), a late and lesser scientific romance, is best placed among the utopist books. In this fantasia on the change of scale in human affairs which Wells had predicted in *Anticipations*, two scientists manufacture Herakleophorbia, the food of the gods, which stimulates growth to six or seven times the normal. Norman Nicholson, while calling it the last vintage Wellsian scientific romance, one combining the best features of his imagination and gift for realism, caricature and character, nevertheless asserts that Wells had never used "a more absurd image for [his] dream of Utopia than that of these monstrous cases of teleological gigantism." [10]

By the curious accident in time stressed in Chapter Four in the discussion of "The Country of the Blind"—a phenomenon unlikely in any other author—*A Modern Utopia,* Wells's clarion call for a ruling hierarchy to make his New Republic hum, and *Kipps,* the author's imperishable monument to inferior, second-class human material, appeared in the same year, 1905. That the two warring tendencies gnawing at Wells's artistic soul should see the light of day within six months of each other is ample testament to the control, at least at this early stage, under which Wells held the demands of artist and polemicist. *A Modern Utopia* crystallizes Wells's mounting inclination to think less and less in terms of individualities like Kipps. "No less than a planet will serve the purpose of a modern Utopia," he writes near the beginning of *A Modern Utopia.* ". . . A state powerful enough to keep isolated under modern conditions would be powerful enough to rule the world. . . . World-state, therefore, it must be" (p. 13).

And what of the Artie Kippses—even those supremely ordinary aspects so extolled by C. E. M. Joad in Wells—in the super-state of the future? Wells might answer obliquely with these words from *First and Last Things*: ". . . there is no being, but a universal *becoming* of individualities. . . ." [11] Whatever is implicit in this almost casual statement of the rationale of utopia—Wells's credo for the last half of his life—it serves notice more clearly than any single passage in his writings of the approaching defection of the novelist to the Messianic world planner.

However questionable as a work of literary art, *A Modern Utopia* falls definitely in the Classic tradition of speculative utopias. Wells's rough equivalents of Plato's guardians are the Samurai, a superior class which by intelligence and good will may be made a ruler caste. The Samurai, drawn from the Japanese word for military knighthood (the Russo-Japanese War had made the term familiar to the English-speaking public), would wear distinctive dress, have a bible of their own selected from the inspiring literature of all ages, and spend at least a week of every year in absolute solitude in the wilderness as a sort of restorative of Emersonian self-reliance (as noted in Chapter Seven, Trafford and his wife Marjorie were to extend in *Marriage* the Samurai ideal to a year in a Labrador tent). "A curious conception [Wells's utopia] was," writes Edwin E. Slosson; "a combination of Puritanism and Bushido, of Fourier and St. Francis, of Bacon's Salomon's House, Plato's philosophers ruling the republic, and Cecil Rhodes's secret order of millionnaires ruling the world." [12]

Wells's utopia is a far cry from Thomas More's virtue and moderation or William Morris's poetic unrestraint made workable by invariable right will. Wells's vision of attainable perfection is always slightly jarred by the inevitable perspective of heroes like Benham in *The Research Magnificent* whose unworldly idealism is defeated by worldly circumstances. Thus Wells departs from belief in man as essentially noble and rational and finds refuge in knowledge and science, organization and management—in George Ponderevo's trust in his battleship at the end of *Tono-Bungay*.

The enfranchising of a head-man species remained, for better or worse, the permanent hope of Wells. The Samurai loom not only as the instruments for his utopian blueprint but are the major inhabitants of all his novels after *Tono-Bungay*. Remington, Capes, Trafford—he, especially—Britling, and Clissold are, each in his way, human projections of the ideals generalized in the Samurai. With the exception of Britling, whose characterization benefits from the empathy a war provides among all concerned in it, none of these personages ever emerges as anything but a spokesman for the idea so dear to Wells's heart: "being" is nothing; "becoming," everything.

No effort would be needed to show how the idealized Trafford of *Marriage*—"the portrait," according to Maugham, "of the man H.G. thought he was, added to the man he would have liked to be" [13]—arose from the underfed poet in Mr. Polly; or, with Wells himself, how the New Republican Samurai caught hold of the imagination of the man who almost lived out his life as a tradesman. Wells endowed his Samurai with the absolute in personal efficiency and orderliness. They are antiseptic, quite without credibility. In assuring that they were innocent of the quality Wells disliked most of all—muddle—he drained them of life. If the Samurai of *A Modern Utopia* provide a logical stepping-stone from the fumblingly real world of Artie Kipps and Mr. Polly to the neatly tiered world of Remington and Trafford, there is an irony lurking behind the transformation. The Samurai of the later novels become dogged by problems, not so much of mankind but of men. Remington's political career is destroyed when he leaves his wife for a more congenial attachment; Stratton in *The Passionate Friends* carries on a doomed romance with a married woman.

The fictional personifications of the utopian supermen are *of* the world in their problems, if not in Wells's delineation of them. But, in his zeal to imagine what the world *ought* to be, Wells deliberately blinds himself to what it *is*. The society forecast in *A Modern Utopia* is unreal. Although Wells is nowhere more visionary and although his vision is a noble belief, André Maurois holds that "the world of flesh and blood, the world of soil and stone is not like that. . . . Plans beyond numbering are applicable in Utopia; on earth, we must live day to day. Equilibrium could only be a stopping-place. Such is the lot of humanity." [14]

III   The World Set Free (*1914*)

As early as 1905, then, an insistent part of Wells's mind was firmly committed to world state-ism. He adamantly refused to concede anything to the other part which had produced the dread intimations of the scientific romances and was even then germinating such novels as *The New Machiavelli, Marriage,* and *The Passionate Friends,* books in which such Wellsian alter egos as Remington, Trafford, and Stratton come to grief because of human egotism and passion.

Just before the outbreak of World War I, Wells published an astoundingly prophetic though badly disjointed utopian work called *The World Set Free.* Not the first novel in which Wells recorded a disastrous world war, the conflict differed in degree if not in kind from *The War in the Air* in that it liberates the race from all obsessions and entanglements which impede moral and material growth. The artisan of world reconstruction is a kind of Albert Schweitzer-with-portfolio, a prominent member of the World Education Committee named Marcus Karenin. Karenin, like so many of those who have tasted of Wells's food of the gods, expires at the end of the novel but not before he, with a wave of his hand "toward the dark sky above the mountain crests," forecasts the end of human travail by an infinite modification of man to eliminate "the obstinacy of egotism":

"The next sciences to yield great harvests now will be psychology and neural physiology [announces Karenin]. These perplexities of the situation between man and woman . . . egotism . . . these are temporary troubles, the issue of our own times. Suddenly all these differences that seem so fixed will dissolve, all these incompatibles will run together, and we shall go on to mould our bodies and our bodily feelings and personal reactions as boldly as we begin now to carve mountains and set the seas in their places and change the currents of the winds." (p. 242)

The World Set Free might not be worth more than passing mention except for its astonishingly accurate forecast of an atomic Armageddon. The war, recorded in a mythical autobiographical novel, dated 1970, as having occurred during "the middle decades of the twentieth century," becomes world-wide. Paris, Berlin, East

London, Chicago, and other great cities are made uninhabitable by the dropping of atomic bombs. Earlier, Wells conceived of splitting the atoms of a rare, little-known metal. Karenin, the scientist-teacher so dear to Wells's heart, holds before his unbelieving class a flask containing fourteen ounces of uranium oxide and says: "If at a word in one instant I could suddenly release the energy of the atoms in this bottle it would blow us and everything about us to fragments; if I could turn it into the machinery that lights this city it could keep Edinburgh brightly lit for a week" (p. 23). A few pages later comes this near-direct hit: "It was in 1953 when the first atomic energy induced radio-activity into the sphere of industrial machinery, and its first general use was to replace the steam engine in electrical generating stations" (p. 37).

Wells held no illusions about the salutary effect of atomic power on humans: "In the year 1955 the suicide rate for the United States of America quadrupled any previous record. There was an enormous increase also in violent crime throughout the world. The thing had come upon an unprepared humanity; it seemed as though human society was to be smashed by its own magnificent gains" (p. 41).

It should be pointed out here, as Professor Warren W. Wagar and Anthony West have stated, that the long-range benevolence of science as viewed in *The World Set Free* is strongly diluted by Wells in subsequent utopist books. He never forgot the limitations of the scientific imagination as he had depicted it in a number of early short stories about absent-minded scientists: in *The Invisible Man*, Griffin turns into a murderer; in *The Island of Dr. Moreau*, Moreau's megalomania threatens the order of the natural world; and in *The First Men in the Moon*, Cavor knows how to resist gravity but presents war to the Grand Lunar as a possible solution to earthly problems. In perhaps Wells's finest idea-novel, *The Undying Fire*, Job Huss monologizes endlessly against the supremacy of old-fashioned rationalism as he argues that science solves nothing among men who have failed in their responsibilities in the ethical sphere.

Scientists, Wells wrote somewhat later, are paralyzed by specialization. The Open Conspiracy leading to a world state needs "the man of more general intelligence and wider purpose. The company of scientific men is less like a host of guiding angels than like a swarm of marvelous bees—endowed with stings—which must be hived and cherished and multiplied. . . ." [15]

IV   Men Like Gods (*1923*)

By far the most sanguine, at least in appearance, of all Wells's utopian novels is *Men Like Gods,* the last to be discussed in any detail. If Wells's one-hundred-plus volumes were to be arranged in left-to-right order—from funeral dirge to spritely pastorale— the work on the far right would undoubtedly be *Men Like Gods.* A recent biographer, Antonina Vallentin, goes so far as to call the novel "a fairy story that Wells told himself on paper." [16] Mr. Barnstaple, the invariable Wellsian, has reached a point of no return. To avoid a nervous breakdown, he slips away from home and family, not unlike Lionel Wallace in Wells's early story, "The Door in the Wall." Suddenly he finds himself in the center of Utopia, a paradise even beyond the expectations of the man who had created a modern utopia two decades earlier. The new Eden makes no concession to a hierarchy; there are no Samurai to guide the new order. Barnstaple encounters a world of wise, beautiful people, who live in perfect harmony with nature and their fellow men. They possess unabashed innocence, too, as shown by their clothing—nature's own—a factor which, according to Madame Vallentin, gave much trouble to the illustrator appointed by the Hearst press, which bought the serial rights.

The intrusion of earth dwellers causes near panic in Utopia. At times the book becomes wildly comic, yet always with an underlying note of melancholy. The book had its *roman-à-clef* undertones, for it was a rare Wells novel during his middle period that did not carry real-life counterparts of the main characters:

There is the Catholic priest, bursting with indignation against a world where churches are no longer built and marriages no longer celebrated; the Utopians consider that his indignation springs from an unhealthy and disordered sexual imagination. There is the conservative politician, an enlightened philosopher: even a miracle is hardly enough to lead his thoughts out of their beaten track. . . . There is the statesman, vehement and volatile, reactionary and reckless, who looks upon the Utopians, with their peace and harmony, as degenerate weaklings. There is the monocled aesthete, lionized in London drawing rooms, who is quite at a loss when faced with genuine beauty. There are the high financier, who has sold his conscience and bought a title; the American movie magnate, who has stolen other people's inventions; the cocky, chauvinistic Frenchman, who still demands, on this Utopian soil, appreciation of the tremendous sacrifices made by France in the cause of civilization.[17]

Wells takes a page from his Martian invasion. Like the invaders of *The War of the Worlds,* the Utopians have no acquired resistance to the illnesses which earth-bred microbes are likely to cause. The mortals—intruders in Utopia—are placed in quarantine. Thereupon, the reckless statesman, dreaming of a universal empire, declares war on the Utopians. Warned by Barnstaple, the only earthling who appreciates their noble world, the Utopians crush the revolt; and, by repeating the atomic experiment which has put them into contact with another universe, they send the mortals back to earth. Barnstaple alone grieves at the loss of Eden —a place where such things as constraints, supreme authority, and police methods are unknown.

Warren W. Wagar, in possibly the finest assessment ever written of Wells as utopographer, concludes that it was H. G. Wells's persistent use of the utopian device, even after civilization had been jolted by World War I, that drew the critics' fire.[18] The majority of the intellectuals scoffed at what they took to be Wells's rose-colored glasses through which he saw, as his shape of things to come, men becoming like gods. Aldous Huxley, grandson of Wells's great mentor, began *Brave New World* as a short-story parody of *Men Like Gods.*[19]

However, Anthony West demurs from this verdict against his father. Wells's detractors, he avers, have missed the supreme irony of *Men Like Gods.* This irony is subtly implicit in the explanation of how Mr. Barnstaple could encounter another universe simply by taking a turn off a familiar road:

Wonder took possession of Mr. Barnstaple's mind. That dear world of honesty and health was beyond the utmost boundaries of our space, utterly inaccessible to him now for evermore; and yet as he had been told it was but one of countless universes that move together in time, that lie against one another, endlessly, like the leaves of a book. And all of them are as nothing in the endless multitudes of systems and dimensions that surround them. "Could I but rotate my arm out of the limits set to it," one of the Utopians had said to him, "I could thrust it into a thousand universes." (p. 323)

The Utopia where men are like gods is, West asserts, but another play in Wells's fifty-year lark with the Fourth Dimension. The earth and Utopia, in terms of a time scheme, are out of joint with one another. The fairy-story aspect of *Men Like Gods* is deliberate on Wells's part: life, as Barnstaple and the other earthlings encounter it, is, in reality, a vacation from life; the novel poses a clash between the human condition and an impossible ideal. "The Utopians are special creations . . . designed simply to evade the truth about human nature," writes Anthony West. "Their triumphs take place in a meaningless free zone in which all reality with which men have to deal is absent. This Utopia could exist for human beings only if the intellect could change the essential nature of reality." [20]

Wells, in what is virtually his last utopian satire, is at the same point he had been in his first one a quarter-century before. Two English monarchs had intervened since he wrote *When the Sleeper Wakes* two years before the death of Victoria. However, his message had not really changed: any valid prospectus which does not take into account humanity as it is—fallible, capable of kindness and courage, folly and cruelty—remains, for all its nobility of vision, an empty dream. The overplanning that had dried up civilization in a desert of machinery in *The Sleeper* can no more save a civilization of men, as the Wells of *Tono-Bungay* and *The New Machiavelli* knew it, than the rose-colored glasses which had enabled a world of godlike men to be seen, but never for a moment believed, in Wells's valedictory utopia.

V The Outline of History (1920)

Although everything about Wells's thinking, especially after World War I, bears the stamp of utopism, the urgency of twentieth-century affairs increasingly obsessed him. "Modern civilization is like an aeroplane in mid-air," he has his autobiographical protagonist in *The World of William Clissold* declare, "an aeroplane with one sole, imperfect engine which is popping and showing many signs of distress." There was little time to make the aerodrome. As he wrote in his seventy-second year—in 1937—"in the race between education and catastrophe, catastrophe is winning." [22] At one point in *Men Like Gods,* Mr. Barnstaple looks pityingly at one of the invaders of Utopia and exhorts him, "Given decent ideas you might have been very different from what you are. If I had been your schoolmaster—But it's too late now" (p. 219).

With the immediate anxieties of war ended in 1918, H. G. Wells moved more directly than any other writer of his time from the theory to the practice of educating the world. Seen in retrospect, *The Outline of History* and its two companion works (*The Science of Life,* 1931, and *The Work, Wealth and Happiness of Mankind,* 1932) are the natural consequence of a mind imbued with blotting out obsolete ideas, loyalties, and prejudices—all those things, in fact, which moored the great mass of people to allegiances of lesser moment than world federation and its corollary, world integration of ideas. Wells quickly saw that mass education rather than a world revolution was the key to at least a partial realization of his dream. Perhaps the world has not seen so colossal a one-man effort in behalf of popular propagandizing toward a private goal as that embodied by H. G. Wells in *The Outline of History.*

Professor Carl Becker, in his profoundly fair appraisal of *The Outline,* observes that, in striving to produce a mass awareness to the force of history, the book may well turn out to be, if not history, an action that has helped to make history. He places Wells in the company of Voltaire, and he defines their kinship by quoting a letter written by Diderot in 1760 to Voltaire apropos of the latter's *Essai sur les Moeurs:*[23] "Other historians relate facts to inform us of facts. You relate them in order to excite in our hearts a profound hatred of lying, ignorance, hypocrisy, superstition, fanaticism, tyranny; and this anger remains, even after the memory of the facts has disappeared."

As Wells grew older, he increasingly relied on generalization and synthesis; and he discarded altogether isolated events and disconnected details. It was this characteristic that made of Wells a species of Higher Journalist who wisely understood, at the opposite pole from the day-to-day "glut of occurrences" of newspapers, what the Present really meant. He made some mistakes—especially, as Orwell has complained, with modern dictators—but, for the most part, his disregard of all those puffed-up "moments of destiny" and their protagonists gave him a wider grasp. He tried to look at Today from the viewpoints of Yesterday and Tomorrow. In that spirit he essayed the heady summit of world history.

That he himself should not only sketch out how the job of writing the history of the world should be done but do it hardly occurred to Wells at first. He embodied his idea of a need for "general history" in a pamphlet *History Is One* (1919) which, according to Professor Wagar, employs the same arguments as those of Arnold J. Toynbee in *A Study of History*.[24] The work was to be a composite Gibbon, brought up to date, with Eastern Asia included. Wells conceived of a symposium of authoritative historians producing a broad but compact synthesis, with massive formulations replacing the counterpoint of chance events that, for him, spoiled the Old History. But Wells saw this plan as impossible because historians "lived in an atmosphere of mutual restraint. They would not dare to do anything so large, for fear of incidental slips and errors. They were unused to any effective cooperation and their disposition would be all towards binding together a lot of little histories by different hands, and calling the binding a synthesis. . . ."[25] Wells was already anticipating that specialists would object to his history on grounds similar in kind to those on which artists like Henry James objected to his novels: his preference always to subordinate the means to the end.

So it was that H. G. and Jane Wells decided in 1918 that the world-famous novelist could afford a year's work exclusively on a précis of history. What started as an essay on the sources and vicissitudes of the idea of European unity since the Caesars grew entirely out of hand into a universal history of prodigious proportions. Wells buttressed his own expanded notes by calling in a corps of specialists to be advisers on his reading and sources of information. Each region, each period, had its authority to counsel him. J. F. Horrabin, the illustrator, became a collaborator. Each chapter was first drafted by Wells; multiple copies were made and sent out to all possible helpers, who wrote, commented, and slashed. Wells then sat down, "chastened and instructed, amidst these mutilated and butchered duplicates," to write afresh. He reserved to himself the rights of private judgment. The 1920 edition is replete with footnote controversies between generalist

Wells and the specialist aides. For example, Ernest Barker's violent disagreement on Wells's low estimate of Napoleon survived as a footnote from Barker: "Put me down as of the opposite opinion." [26]

As might be expected of the author of biology texts, of a story like *The Island of Dr. Moreau*, and of a bookshelf of scientific romances, H. G. Wells was most at home writing of pre-history. The same genius that evoked the unforgettable dawn on the moon or the vision of the year thirty million in *The Time Machine* served him well in dealing with pristine eras. A few years later, in his fictional counterpart of *The Outline*, the cumbersome but worthwhile *World of William Clissold* (1926), Wells acknowledged his predilection for writing pre-history.[27] Clissold confesses that "No other part of history so interests me as the opening chapter before the documents begin. There is no excessive presentation of persons and personal names; egotism has left nothing of persons and personal names; egotism has left nothing but defaced monuments and disconnected boats, and we seem to come nearer to the realities of human life than we do in a later age when kings and princes and their policies monopolize the foreground." [28]

Until a recent objection was registered to the pre-history chapters by novelist William Golding, whose debt to Wells's *Island of Dr. Moreau* was noted in Chapter Three, most critics of *The Outline* have been willing to accept the first seven chapters, which covered the origins of life through the development of early man to the invention of language, as, in the words of Professor Becker, "the account . . . of a man who has mastered the subject well enough to understand the evidence [who] . . . in the spirit of the scientist . . . with no special thesis to defend and no practical aims to further . . . approaches his subject [in the first chapters]." [29]

However, in his chapter on Neanderthal Man, Wells writes that "this species of men was accumulating a dim tradition, and working out its limited possibilities. Its thick skull imprisoned its brain, and to the end it was low-browed and brutish." [30] Twenty-five years later, Golding took issue.[31] He produced in *The Inheritors* (1954) a parable about the death of the last Neanderthal man at the hands of human beings whose ruthless cruelty and cunning are more truly "brutish" things.

[128]

Certainly the Wells who wrote *The Island of Dr. Moreau* believed that man intrinsically is as much a savage today as was the Neanderthal brute. Morality, in the thesis put forth by Wells in *Dr. Moreau,* is simply, as Henkin has said, the padding of social and emotional habits by which society keeps the round Neanderthal savage in the square hole of the civilized state.[32] But, by the time Wells was writing about recorded history for his monumental *Outline,* he was committed by his public image to a view of civilized humanity as a knight on a white charger winning in cosmic conflict with brute nature. Here T. H. Huxley's great question about mankind's ability to survive the blind impulses of nature was given affirmative answer by the impressionable student grown into a middle-aged apostle of scientific materialism. Only an emergent intelligence like man's could blossom in nature's luxuriant but potentially destructive garden. Out of humanity's survival Wells drew the whole plan and meaning of history. If intelligence could create civilized communities at the dawn of recorded history, then certainly, Wells insisted, history was essentially the endeavor of intelligence to bring all civilized communities under conscious control.

Wells's history—with its insights, the broad sweep of a superiorly equipped overseer, and its felicity of style—is an unparalleled work until the point where Wells-with-a-mission gets ahead of the Wells-with-a-story. When he leaves the safely remote civilizations and the early steps in the advancement of the science of learning; when he approaches political history—with conquerors, kings and statesmen on center stage; when his narrative touches on events still relatively close to the immediate past, especially the cataclysmic war just ended, then the loving patience of the guidepost builder succumbs to the exasperation of a partisan spectator.

It is not within the province of this study to detail the storm of criticism which accompanied popular acceptance of *The Outline.* Certainly the long, heated diatribes which Wells and his old Anglo-Catholic adversary Hilaire Belloc exchanged over *The Outline's* interpretation of the origins of Christianity have no place here. In the United States, at that time undergoing sweeping proposals for revitalizing the teaching of history, such New Historians as Professors Becker, J. Salwyn Schapiro, and Carlton J. H. Hayes reviewed the book more conscientiously than their English brethren who either ignored it or discounted it with faint mention. The New Historians, according to an exhaustive investigation of American reviews by Professor Wagar, "all found serious fault with Wells's methods, sources, and content but applauded his scale of objections and his objectives." [33] Hayes spoke for most when he wrote that Wells "Was making the world safe for historians. Henceforth professors will not fear to walk where Mr. Wells has leaped, and eventually one of them or a group of them will produce a history of man in the universe that will be as sound and reliable as the 'Outline' before us is inaccurate and impressionistic." [34] His old friends from the Fabian days, Bernard Shaw and Graham Wallas, liked *The Outline;* and Harold Laski called it "the greatest public service the universities have been rendered in a generation." [35]

The book, as noted in an earlier connection, fortified Wells's popular reputation—made his a household name with people younger than the generation which matured during World War I. Although Wells noted in his autobiography that "over two million copies . . . have been sold since 1919," [36] the commercial success of the *Outline* has been far out of proportion to its probable influence. Aldous Huxley's view that the work reached the wrong people for it to be lastingly influential is well-known.[37] Even Wells had no illusions:

In various formats we sold over a million at a great pace. I do not think that more than a minute percentage of that tremendous issue was ever more than glanced at. I doubt if more than two or three thousand were ever attentively read. It was bought and stowed away. When the topic of this H. G. Wells, who was trying to tell the world something, came up, the good Anglo-Saxon world could say: 'We know all about H.G.W. We've got an illustrated copy of his *Outline* in the library and the Christmas before last we made it our gift book to all our friends'.[38]

Most libraries contain the black-jacketed early edition of *The Outline* or possibly the tri-volumed edition that brought the story up to the start of World War II. The book, according to Professor Wagar, "became oppressively fashionable in the middle class [but] in mid-century [it] is mostly a dust-collector.[39]

Wells's didactic instinct aside—the fact that, as Hartley Grattan rightly observes, he proposed to rewrite history as propaganda for his world state—*The Outline of History* is undoubtedly a tremendously effective piece of public education in behalf of the plea to read history as a testament to the necessity of Oneness:

> One cannot foretell the surprises or disappointments the future has in store. Before this chapter of the World State can begin fairly in our histories, other chapters as yet unsuspected may still need to be written, as long and as full of conflict as our account of the growth and rivalries of the Great Powers and the insurrection of gangster totalitarianism. . . . Human history becomes more and more a race between education and catastrophe. . . .
> Life begins perpetually. Gathered together at last under the leadership of man, the student-teacher of the universe, unified, disciplined, armed with the secret powers of the atom, and with knowledge as yet beyond dreaming, Life, for ever dying to be born afresh, for ever young and eager, will presently stand upon earth as upon a footstool, and stretch out its realm against the stars.[40]

The writer of those words may have been without all spiritual values, as one of his severest critics asserts; but he was not without a faith. What makes declarations such as these closing words from his best-known work appear so shallow to scoffing intellectuals is that they stem from the soul, not of the artist, but of the pamphleteer—albeit the inspired pamphleteer of a commendable pamphlet. *The Outline of History* was, in fact, a conscious effort toward a reassurance Wells could not feel in his heart after the disenchantment of World War I. A message delivered by the propagandist in Wells to the artist, the work sought to justify the former to the latter. But the justification was as empty as the God which Mr. Britling created to enable him to endure the war.

For a dying sage was to write, only a few years after he tacked on his optimistic postscript to the latest revision of *The Outline,* that "this world is at the end of its tether. The end of everything we call life is close at hand and cannot be evaded. . . . The stars in their courses [had turned against man] and he has to give place to some other animal better adapted to face the fate that closes in more and more swiftly upon mankind."[41] These words, among the last published by Wells, reveal not the disappointment at a world that failed to heed his counsels of perfection but a realization that he had betrayed himself. Wells realized from the vantage of a gigantic production of temporary dikes against floods—seen and foreseen—that he had turned aside from his artist's duty of describing the world as he knew it to be. In his seventies, while still writing pamphlets for world state-ism and when visiting Somerset Maugham at his Riviera villa, Wells ran his thumb down the long ranks of his books. When Wells spoke, the words were as candid as any he had ever uttered: "All dead," he said. "Dead as mutton." [42]

CHAPTER 10

Wells at the End of His Tether

THE phenomenal success of *The Outline of History* hastened the demise of the novelist. Wells promptly enlisted, for the gigantic task of educating the world out of outdated ideas and loyalties, two more omnibus volumes; and each in its way is as ambitious a work as the *Outline*. With his biologist son, G. P. Wells, and Julian Huxley he sought to provide the average man with all he could want to know about biological discovery, about his body, about the origins of life. *The Science of Life* (1931), published in his sixty-fifth year, was the result. Then, without so much as a breather, Wells threw himself into the production of the first comprehensive summary "of the whole of mankind working or playing or unemployed . . . to supersede the vague generalizations on which Marxism rests and [to] concentrate and synthesize all those confused socialist and individualist theorizings of the nineteenth century which still remain as the unstable basis of our economic experiments." [1] *The Work, Wealth & Happiness of Mankind* (1932) completed a vast trilogy which alone, according to Sir Arthur Salter, "would have justified [Wells's] title to be the greatest public teacher of our time." [2]

I *Educator of the Public*

It was to this task of educating the public that, for the last twenty-five years of his life, Wells subordinated every other purpose in life. *Joan and Peter* (1918) and *The Undying Fire* (1919) are the last of his novels to pledge even token allegiance to non-doctrinaire art. The first, a book Wells thought much superior to *Mr. Britling*, joins almost successfully its author's increasing preoccupation with education and that attention to characterization with which the creator of Kipps could still clothe a novel. Joan and Peter, two orphans brought up by an empire-builder uncle named Oswald, are thoroughly believable as children; but the feeling persists that Wells regards them more as laboratory specimens than as humans. Wells's central concern is how young people, miseducated by formal education in preparatory schools ("like trying to graft mummy-steak on living flesh . . . boiling fossils for soup"), can adjust themselves to the great war and to adulthood and marriage. The tragedy, as Uncle Oswald (and Wells) saw it, was that young people under King Edward, without clear aims or a sense of responsibilities in a shrinking world, should have been brought face to face with a war.

The Undying Fire, the most spiritual of all Wells's novels, has already been discussed. Job Huss was the dedicated schoolmaster of the "advanced" type school from which Joan and Peter were abducted by a Victorian fossil of an aunt. R. W. Sanderson, the headmaster of Oundle, to whom Wells sent his sons at the outbreak of war, was the living embodiment of Job Huss and virtually the only teacher who escaped Wells's wrath. In *The Story of a Great Schoolmaster* (1924), Wells paid tribute to him.

The World of William Clissold (1926) is, as the modern Existentialist Colin Wilson observes, well worth reading,[3] but it is not a novel. Clissold is a tapestry woven from strands of Trafford— the pure scientist who deserted science for business; of Teddy Ponderevo, for Clissold has become wealthy; but, above all, of H. G. Wells, who had himself settled with a mistress in the South of France. Like Remington in *The New Machiavelli,* Clissold has come to rest after a vigorous period that included a scandal. However, fifteen years have elapsed between Remington and Clissold. Wells is no longer concerned with the effects of human irrationality. Clissold is doing nothing less than planning the Open Conspiracy which will bring World State out of present confusions. The book compounds the tendencies of *Mr. Britling,* written a decade earlier. Contemporary names are cited in profusion. In fact, were the book cast as a memoir of Wells at sixty, it might be considered an invaluable record of where, to the spokesman for faith in a progressively scientific future, the world was heading between the two great wars. "Indeed, it is possible to open it anywhere and be stimulated by the brilliant journalism," writes Norman Nicholson, who cites a short biography of Lord Northcliffe;

an essay on the development of advertising in England; and, naturally, a dissertation on public schools.[4]

D. H. Lawrence, with whom Wells got along better than most of Lawrence's contemporaries, recognized more forcefully than anyone of comparable stature that Clissold buried Wells as a novelist.[5] The book interested Shaw for another reason. For him, it proved Wells had at last come to know what "gentry" means.[6] But Wells could not, or would not, Shaw said, act the part. This observation, one he never elaborated on, is much more perceptive than even Shaw knew. The Wellsian persona that inhabits all the novels after *Clissold* is a man who finds no peace despite enormous material success; like Sir Richmond in *Secret Places of the Heart* (1922), this man is "entirely capable of being faithful to an idea, and entirely incapable of being faithful to his wife." World planners like Clissold are unable to resolve the chaos of their personal life. Promiscuous living involves for such as Sir Richmond (and Wells) no detriment to social standing or career as it did in the days of Remington's fall. Richmond (and Wells) availed himself of the conventional ways of getting around social conventions —the ways of gentry; he had an artist girl-friend whom he referred to as "my mistress," a far cry from the earlier Wellsian heroes and heroines who regarded marriage as a pact which, if broken, could destroy a career (Remington in *The New Machiavelli*) or bring suicide (Lady Mary Justin in *The Passionate Friends*).

II *Despair at Sixty*

With the death in 1927 of his wife, Jane, H.G.W.'s personal problems all but inundated him. The reflection of a worsening private condition is seen in novel after novel in which the protagonist expresses the idea of being squeezed by a muddled world. Invariably, each hero bears a replica of part of Wells's own moral history. In *Clissold,* the scientist hero, like Wells, is sixty and distressed by the idea of death: "I do not want to go yet. I am sorry to have so little time before me. I wish before the ebb carries me right out of things that I could know more—and know better. I came into the world with a clutter of protest; my mind is still haunted by protesting questions too vague for me to put into any form that would admit of an answer." [7]

In *Apropos of Dolores* (1938), the hero tells of contemplating suicide: ". . . I saw my life as an inextricable muddle, and I repudiated suicide perhaps because it presented itself as an effort too troublesome to attempt, or . . . because I was under obligation to various people . . . not to confess that the life they had thought worthwhile and found some comfort in, was a failure." [8] In *Brynhild* (1937), the hero, Mr. Rowland Place, awakens to "a world of cheerless realities, persistent and inexorable" in which "like so many men who make their way to positions of importance in the world of thought and letters [he] was a man of acute sensibilities and incessant anxieties." [9]

The mood became so overwhelming that by 1932, when Wells began a prelude to his autobiography, he revealed the tissue of despair his life had become:

I need freedom of mind. I want peace for work. I am distressed by immediate circumstances. My thoughts and work are encumbered by claims and vexations and I cannot see any hope of release from them; any hope of a period of serene and beneficent activity, before I am overtaken altogether by infirmity and death. I am in a phase of fatigue and of that discouragement which is a concomitant of fatigue, the petty things of to-morrow skirmish in my wakeful brain, and I find it difficult to assemble my forces to confront this problem which paralyses the proper use of myself. [10]

This despair is more than that of an old man. Wells, at sixty-five, was in more robust health than during his youth and early manhood. What dogged him was evidently a reaction against the notion that absolute self-enjoyment was the aim of life. He had stressed this goal in *Men Like Gods*. In his later testamental novels—climaxed by his autobiography—he is a man full of doubt about the Machine as a purveyor of happiness and about material comfort as contributing anything to the creative will. A passage like the following could only have been written by one dubious of the efficacy of human effort to find an Elysium of intellectual activity as opposed to the tiresome necessities of everyday:

Our lives are threaded with [a] desperate effort to disentangle ourselves, to get a Great Good place of our own, and work freely.

None of us really get there, perhaps there is no *there* anywhere to get to. . . . We never do the work that we imagine to be in us. . . . Some of us . . . let everything else slide, live in garrets and hovels, borrow money unscrupulously, live on women. . . . exploit patronage, accept pensions. But even the careless life will not stay careless. It has its own frustrations and chagrins.[11]

This speaker is not the incurable optimist, ever confident of the eventual triumph of common sense. It is a man full of Existentialist forebodings who, in a host of novels and tracts after World War I, refused to look fully at his world and, by deepening his vision, create books on which his valedictory effort, *Mind at the End of Its Tether* (1945) could rest rather than, as is the case, fall harshly.

Thus the gradual return of Wells to the pessimism of his creative period can easily be seen even in an idea-novel like *William Clissold* and his massive Autobiography. Anthony West, in perhaps the most moving personal memoir ever built around the aging Wells, discusses the impossibility of reconciling the dark world that his father actually inhabited with the place that his bubbling forecasts and avuncular image as apostle of progress seemed to promise.[12] The manner of nearly all Wells's journalism—and that includes the three massive outlines—was best described by Cyril Connolly as "button-holing." The tone is invariably evangelical. The spirit is that of "the hard-sell," and the thing being sold is usually some current enthusiasm of today which will be replaced or repudiated tomorrow. H. L. Mencken lost his respect for a once brilliant novelist who sold out to capricious concerns of the moment.[13] The novelist's view, he wrote,

must regard the internal workings and meanings of existence and not merely its superficial appearances. A novelist must draw on life from some secure rock, viewing it in a definite perspective, interpreting it upon an ordered plan. Even if he hold (as Conrad does, and Dreiser, and Hardy, and Anatole France) that it is essentially meaningless, he must at least display that meaninglessness with reasonable clarity and consistency. Wells shows no such solid and intelligible attitude. He is too facile, too enthusiastic, too eager to teach today what he learned yesterday.

This study can but touch on the undeniable violence that Wells's strivings to obviate the Shavian "time-lag" did to his work. He once chided Julian Huxley on his failure to produce copy for *The Science of Life* at deadline.[14] It is doubtful if Wells ever missed a deadline in that private schema which he, after the manner of his earliest alter ego, Mr. Lewisham, formulated. It called for every accord and discord to produce a book. If it was a tenet of philosophy—his World State, for example—it could produce several dozen books, as that overriding ideology assuredly did. The production of a superjournalist thus driven can be, as it was with Wells, unparalleled; but it is not the method of the writer of books that last beyond their original impulse. Wells, perhaps necessarily in the Shavian scheme of things, gave himself during his mature years to hordes of time-consuming projects that could only end by taking from him those precious periods of meditation during which ideas are, in the manner of Landor's poem, warmed before the fire, savored in tranquility, and brought to light with the infinite care art bestows. His preoccupations with the Fabians in his early years, the League of Nations in his middle period, and a world encyclopedia in his final period may be cited. He was a man of nine lives ever in search of a tenth.

III *Wells in the Kremlin*

As the successor in 1935 to John Galsworthy as president of the world writing fraternity, P.E.N., and as a man who became *ex officio* a statesman of letters, Wells was the precise opposite of the artist alienated from world affairs. During the 1930's he made no secret of his unbounded admiration for Franklin D. Roosevelt in the United States and for Joseph Stalin in the Soviet Union. Before Stalin, Lenin had said to Wells at the end of their conversation in 1920, "Come back and see us in ten years." [15] That visit had not been satisfactory for Wells who—in common with Shaw, the Webbs, and a host of other Socialist writers—was enchanted by the thought that militant collectivism was being applied and succeeding in the Soviet. For Wells, Russia bore the closest resemblance to his dream of a world state. But after his talk with Lenin, Wells wrote *Russia in the Shadows,* a bitter attack on Marxian economics and Leon Trotsky quoted Lenin as remarking that Wells was impossibly bourgeois.[16]

Wells returned to Russia, not in ten years, but in fourteen. On July 23, 1934, Liberalism and Marxism once more confronted each other across a table in the Kremlin. Lenin had impressed Wells as a great man. The man now opposite him was one who had long aroused his suspicion and prejudice: Stalin. Wells had just come from Washington where he had found in Roosevelt and the New Deal a constructive effort quite congenial to his own Open Conpiracy. In Moscow, he experienced the doctrinaire fixity of view of Marxism. Wells and Stalin talked for almost three hours; the scheduled forty-minute session was extended at Stalin's insistence. During the interview, Wells tried with no success to convince Stalin that large-scale planning—the socialization of industry and transportation—was a concomitant of scientific developments and was going on as much outside the Soviet as inside. Stalin merely stressed the class struggle and refused to see any tie-in between the New Deal and Five-Year Plans.

Wells, the spokesman for a world citizenry, scored only once, but his was a telling shot for individual liberty inconceivable under Stalin:

STALIN: It seems to me, Mr. Wells, that you greatly underestimate the question of political power, that it entirely drops out of your conception. What can those, even with the best intentions in the world, do if they are unable to raise the question of seizing power, and do not possess power. . . . This can only be done by a great class which will take the place of the capitalist class and become the sovereign master as the latter was before. This class is the working class. . . . The transformation of the world is a great, complicated and painful process. For this great task a great class is required. *Big* ships go on long voyages.
WELLS: Yes, but for long voyages a captain and a navigator are required.
STALIN: That is true; but what is first required for a long voyage is a big ship. What is a navigator without a ship? An idle man.
WELLS: The big ship is humanity, not a class.[17]

Stalin countered by charging Wells with believing that all men are good whereas he, Stalin, had reason not to believe in the goodness of the bourgeoisie. Wells answered by extolling the technical intelligentsia as men full of a fervor for revolution: the scientific reorganization of human society.

Wells recorded his disappointment over everything he saw in the Soviet except Pavlov's Institute of Psychological Genetics, which he called "the most significant biological work in the world today actually in progress." [18] His severest disillusionment was reserved for his reunion with an old friend, Maxim Gorky. Wells found in Gorky, whom he had always admired as a fellow outcast and progressive, a kind of totem and an apologist for the state's controlled literature; the outcast had been transformed into a sycophant who called Russia a land at war: a country which could not tolerate opposition from artists within its borders.

IV *Wells at Seventy*

In the fall of 1936, the P.E.N. Club gave a seventieth birthday party for Wells, its illustrious president. He declared he hated being seventy and compared himself to a little boy who, at a grand party, has been given a lot of lovely toys and is spreading them on the floor when his nurse appears and says, "Now Master Bertie, it's getting late. Time you begin to put away your toys." [19]

But Wells was not ready to put away his toys. There was a relatively new one to play with, a kind of "world brain" to which, however incompletely, his three outlines contributed. To win the race with catastrophe, a new kind of encyclopedic education was essential. It would buoy up the listing morale of the human race and set all these confused minds to work in one direction. "We want," H. G. Wells wrote in 1938, "a reconditioned and more powerful Public Opinion. . . . [We want] a World Brain which will replace our multitude of unco-ordinated ganglia, our powerless miscellany of universities, research institutions, literatures with a purpose, national educational systems and the like. . . ." [20]

His was a cold and bookish panacea to be proposed at a time when the West teetered on the edge of World War II. To place his faith in the creating of a citadel of universal knowledge was a shrill whistle in the dark for the man who only a year earlier had given vent to positive despair in *The Anatomy of Frustration* (1936). The book, its title clearly borrowed from Robert Burton's *Anatomy of Melancholy,* intoned clearly what the novels of that period were implying. George Ponderevo's—Trafford's—dream of hitching on to some transcending dream that would redeem life for its baggage of jealousies, cheatings, and self-frustrations is seen to be futile. Wells writes the book in the form of a biography of still another alter ego—Steele—who dies by his own wish; and death is the logical culmination of his despair.

V *Dictators, Not Samurai*

The last ten years of Wells's life need be mentioned only in passing. In 1935, he wrote a scenario based on his utopian novel, *The Shape of Things to Come*. The film, *Things to Come*, was produced by Alexander Korda and starred Raymond Massey and Cedric Hardwicke. It provided millions of young film-goers who had never read him with a celluloid version of the popular image of Wells as architect of the mechanized, scientifically planned order that would follow the Armageddon depicted in the novel. The man who had "invented" tanks, aerial warfare, and the atomic bomb portrayed white-suited air-borne Samurai who would be custodians of the automated world to come. In Germany, even as Wells prepared his scenario, Hitler was writing one of his own; and the Western World was plunging to its own Armageddon.

That Wells knew that disaster was close at hand is indicated by the wry, semi-comic irony of a trio of novels written during the decade before Germany invaded Poland. *Mr. Blettsworthy on Rampole Island* (1928), written as "a caricature of the entire world of humanity," introduces a note of cruelty not found in Wells since *Dr. Moreau;* and it comments also on the Sacco-Vanzetti case. The shipwrecked Blettsworthy is washed up on Rampole Island among cannibals who intrude on the imagination as blatantly as the beasts that Dr. Moreau tried to transform into men. Blettsworthy lives among the savages as a sacred lunatic, like the leaders of the world who so sorely disappointed Wells with their immunity from responsibility to forge a world order.

The Autocracy of Mr. Parham (1930) and *The Holy Terror* (1939) are about dictatorship and reveal once again how events serve to outstep Wells's fiction. Parham is a flamboyant cartoon of the British imperialist who fears Russia but idolizes Mussolini. In a dream, Parham sees himself as dictator of England. He summons his followers to a mass meeting at Albert Hall and harangues an excited crowd in the manner of Il Duce's "i-popoli-d'Italia" speeches of the time. Four years after *Mr. Parham,* Oswald Mosley held a meeting of his black shirts in the same Albert Hall.

Young Rudolf (rhymes with Adolph) in *The Holy Terror* is a tiresome, bad-tempered boy, a fugitive from *Joan and Peter,* who could not overcome his miseducation (as his creator had done). He becomes Rud the dictator. The novel, one of Wells's poorest, has a certain academic interest for the evolution of the Wellsian rebels it tokened. Dr. Moreau, Griffin, Trafford—Wells's early scientists—were exceptional men who drew their fire from a sense of mission stemming from a Huxleyan scientific education. Rudolf's strength lies in his failings. Far from being a member of any élite —Samurai or New Republican—Rud draws his breath in an atmosphere of ignorance, laziness, vulgarity. He becomes "a holy terror" of a megalomaniac by exploiting all that is basest and vile in human nature. When Wells wrote his first books, vengeance— his own as well as those of his fictional alter egos—could still be a virtuoso matter. Griffin ranged the Woking countryside—but alone. In the days of Hitler and Mussolini, the avenger raises armies.

"A day will come," writes Antonina Vallentin, "when future sociologists will find in [*The Holy Terror*] a deal of valuable information about a troubled epoch when men's minds were glad to capitulate—an age of contempt when men renounced their human dignity." [21]

VI Babes in the Darkling Wood (*1940*)

On the eve of World War II, Wells tried to repeat the success of *Mr. Britling* with the novel *Babes in the Darkling Wood.* Then in his seventy-fifth year, he was disenchanted by a world that had failed to heed his counsels. He had watched with stern vigilance the world move farther away from the one active order he had always envisaged. In 1939, Wells's panic at the onset of world war had moved him to revise his most famous short story, "The Country of the Blind," after a third of a century. Then in 1940 he wrote a three-decker novel to assuage the urgency in his heart and mind.

Babes in the Darkling Wood is the poorest work of fiction Wells ever wrote. Instead of some reassuring dedication, such as the kind Maugham was prone to append to his own potboilers of this period, Wells wrote a long justification for the "dialogue novel" which appeared as a foreword to *Babes;* he rehashed his *Fortnightly Review* article of 1911 and added a bitter inveighing against the critics for slighting him.

The novel is not discounted by its form but by its execution. Stripped of its flimsy framework of plot, the book tends in the direction of reporting and of lightly diluted interview technique. It is actually little different from the mass of war journals and correspondents' memoirs, "made" and "compiled" books that flooded the markets during the war years. It is, in the words of F. T. Marsh, "a potpourri of ideas in the form of notes, rough drafts, thinking one's way out loud, presented through mouthpieces all talking more or less alike in dialogues or long monologues." [22]

In this book the reporter Wells took many subjects—education, sex, religion, schools of psychology, Communism—and contrived situations in which "experts" in these fields were able to expound articulately. The novel is best dissected by division into interviews in which characters do not so much move about and function as they talk incessantly. In an unintentional parody of Plato's Socratic Dialogues—a form for which Wells, not surprisingly, expresses great admiration—character after character is produced to state his views in long interviews with an interlocutor.

The two principals—an intellectual young couple who do not talk like young people but as an old man thinks young people talk—discuss in page after page set between quotation marks the need for a mass of human beings to shape the world under a single authority. Then the pair—Stella and Gemini—"interview" a free-lance journalist, a clergyman, a psychotherapist, and finally an omniscient being who seems created in the image of the aging Open Conspirator himself.

Wells once wrote a justification to Frank Swinnerton for assembling an unlikely group for the purpose of airing viewpoints.[23] Whatever his success in earlier novels—*Mr. Britling* and *Clissold* come to mind as books that survived such a contrivance—*Babes in the Darkling Wood* does not. One almost hears the creaking of furniture as Wells "stages" his interviews. These noises mute entirely the ring of reality necessary to the novel. At many points in the dialogue, Wells encounters difficulties experienced by the journalist writing up an interview report. Often the weight of the ideas expressed are such that quotes—or, using Wells's term, "monologues"—cannot carry them adequately. The newswriter resorts to exposition and narrative instead of question and answer. In the interview between Gemini Twain and the clergyman, one finds Wells breaking in to give expositorily the substance of the argument: "And Gemini proceeded to argue, with all the confidence and ready fullness of a brilliant student fresh from his preparation, that the false dichotomy implied in the opposition of material and spiritual was being kept alive by the organized religions in spite of advancing human thought, and it encumbered that advance, and this was the chief cause of the stupefaction of civilization in the present crisis." [24] When this interview is nearly over, Wells makes the Vicar summarize. He gives to the clergyman words that a newspaper journalist, writing his article "straight," would work into his first paragraph. The novel, the next to last he wrote, is the skeleton of thirty years' decomposition of the novelist's art.

Curiously enough, a year later, Wells returned in *You Can't Be Too Careful* (1941) to the characterization of the social misfits— the Kippses and Pollys—he had portrayed in his golden period as novelist. His Edward Albert Tewler is as spiritually starved as Albert Polly, but he does not have Mr. Polly's determination to impose change on his life. Also a victim of dishonest education, Tewler lacks George Ponderevo's zeal to force a link to the Mind of the Race; he deliberately chooses to withdraw into mediocrity. The post-Victorian world creaked under the strain of many tiny rebellions; the world at mid-century walls up the Tewlers in a cage of security: one can't be too careful. This last of Wells's novels carries the same shrill note of warning as his first book a half-century earlier. Wells describes a state of mind that existed on the eve of World War II. "A solid mass of Homo Tewler," writes Madame Vallentin, "was still blocking up all paths toward the future, an impenetrable mass, which perhaps would never awaken to that idea of the cosmopolis that alone could save mankind." [25]

You Can't Be Too Careful came without any preparation just after his unintentional parody of the idea-novel devices he had worked to death for so long and just before he was to give vent to total despair in *Mind at the End of Its Tether*. In the story of

Edward Albert Tewler, Wells saw in the flash of a double-take the quality of the raw material which would have to man the wheel of destiny. The novel proved the last time that H. G. Wells would see the human condition clearly.

Wells lived through the blitz in the middle of a London under bombardment. He refused to leave his home in Hanover Terrace —the one he had purchased in 1935 from Alfred Noyes—and the world press's last pictures of him are those of an adamant Britisher shaking his fist at the invading planes. Elizabeth Bowen tells of calling on Wells late at night at the height of the blitz. A trembling Wells came to the door. "But you shouldn't be frightened at all this," Miss Bowen remarked. "After all you invented it all." Wells looked at her and said: "It's not the bombs, it's the dark. I've been afraid of darkness all my life." [26] Wells suffered a physical breakdown in 1942, from which he never recovered. It was spiritual as well. He lived to see World War II concluded by an atomic blast he had predicted in 1913.

If *You Can't Be Too Careful* had been the final published work of H. G. Wells, there would have been a kind of divine justice about the return of a wayward artist to home port. Instead, his body racked and weakened by a damaged kidney, diabetes, weak heart, and catarrh, he wrote almost until the end. In his seventy-ninth year he published a curious, misanthropic, and disorganized little book which, in its thirty-seven pages, repudiated all he had ever stood for as a writer. A modern Existentialist like Colin Wilson places the pamphlet, *Mind at the End of Its Tether*, beside T. S. Eliot's *Hollow Men* as "the most pessimistic single utterance in modern literature." [27] Wells wrote:

Our universe is not merely bankrupt; there remains no dividend at all; it has not simply liquidated; it is going clean out of existence, leaving not a wrack behind. . . .

The writer sees the world as a jaded world devoid of recuperative power. In the past he has liked to think that man could pull out of his entanglements and start a new creative phase of human living. In the face of our universal inadequacy, that optimism has given place to a stoical cynicism. . . . Ordinary man is at the end of his tether. Only a small, highly adaptable minority of the species can possibly survive. . . .[28]

Wells repudiated his penultimate volume, *'42 to '44*, which contained a doctoral thesis submitted in the twilight of his career to London University. *'42 to '44* had sought to do in World War II what his pamphleteering during the previous war had done: find some reassurance against disaster. But in *Tether* Wells compared those hopes to "the remembered shouts of angry people in a train that has passed and gone forever." [29] In perhaps the most revealing section of his melancholy tract, he turns to deal with the individual, the single human soul he had neglected during his long period of sterility as a novelist:

Whatever dismaying realities our limited reasoning unfolds before us, our normal life is happily one of personal ambitions, affections, generosities, a mixture in nearly every individual of the narrowest prejudices, hates, competitiveness and jealousies with impulses of the most unselfish and endearing quality, bright friendliness, unasked helpfulness; and this, the everyday foreground of our thought will always be sufficiently vivid to outshine any sustained intellectual persuasion. . . . *We live in reference to past experience and not to future events, however inevitable.*[30]

Here Wells seemed to be reducing the fountainhead idea of his life—that *becoming* not *being* is important—to rubble. Elsewhere in the essay Wells constrains readers to regard his final testament as based on scientific fact, objective reality. It would be comforting to agree with Professor Robert P. Weeks that the valedictory pessimism of Wells was largely the cynicism and despair of an old man whose earlier optimism had suffered a long succession of rebuffs.[31] However, as indicated in these pages, the grain of all of Wells's major fiction (and even a bad book like *Babes in the Darkling Wood* has a significant whimpering amidst the brave trumpetings) is strongly skeptical of the forging of any sustained rational program on a large scale when the raw material it would have to deal with is malleable to the point of chaos. Only the single-minded intensity of *Mind at the End of Its Tether*—the degree of its despair—can be taken as surprising. And this new dimension may be said to stem from the urgency of a man under sentence of death.

CHAPTER 11

The Shape of Wells to Come

IT would be easy enough to dismiss H. G. Wells with the comforting pat on the back reserved for those honored as the liberators, not creators, of thought. This accolade was bestowed on him by Bertrand Russell, the last remaining of Wells's contemporaries who fought the good fight with him against that bundle of oppressions to which the term "Victorianism" has been applied.

One might proceed in this keep-off-the-literary-grass campaign against Wells to the high rank accorded to him as teacher. Sir Arthur Salter devoted one of the most moving of all the assessments of Wells to justifying the *New York Times*'s obituary editorial which called the author of *The Outline of History* the "greatest public teacher" of his time. W. Warren Wagar devoted an entire book, formidable in its clear scholarship, to the proposition that H. G. Wells, much more than any other single thinker, created the frame of public mind hospitable to world integration.

No one, to my knowledge, has kept the score of Wells's hits and misses as a prophet. In short stories, scientific romances, and essays written at the time of *Anticipations* (1901), Wells forecast the shape of twentieth-century warfare and the vanishing distinction between soldier and non-combatant; the collectivist organization of the community to secure the highest production efficiency; the coming of specialized motor-ways (he did everything but use the word "arterial"); the emerging of nuclear fission and fusion as features of everyday life.

"Reality has taken a leaf from my book and set itself to supersede me," fretted Wells in 1934 in writing of how Hitler's preliminary didos were outpacing those of his own fictional Mr. Parham in 1930. From the day in 1884 when Wells arrived in London from the rural Home Counties until the last years when he had the courage to remain in London throughout the blitz, he kept his antenna tuned to the vibrations of the contemporary world. On one level *The First Men in the Moon* can be taken as an exact prognostication of automation and *Tono-Bungay*, his best work of fiction, a preview of the coming dominance of advertising and publicity.

It is not easy to say by what special alchemy Wells became the sounding-board for the generation whose middle years were sandwiched between the two great world wars. Certainly, in his appetites and fundamental allegiances, he was completely a simple man. He kept telling people he had a very active second-class mind. Such self-denigrations were half-truths, and Wells knew it. It is doubtful if, in all the history of English literature, there is another instance in which one man brought out in the same year a major novel in the post-Victorian manner like *Kipps* and a triumph of the visionary imagination like *A Modern Utopia*. Wells did it in 1905.

It was Wells's supreme ordinariness that gave him the sympathy with ordinary persons to enable him to write a book like *Kipps*. It places him in direct line of fictional descent from Fielding, from Smollett, from Dickens. But Wells in life built so much out of the plasticity of his Kippses and Pollys that he grew desperately impatient with the slow grind of humanity's wheels. While keeping one ear cocked to the concerns of the Kipps in him, he drew into the other ear false whispers from the lips of the spirit of the times. He came to feel, as his best novel (*Tono-Bungay*) and most insistent credo (*First and Last Things*) show, that only *becoming*, never *being*, was important.

When H. G. Wells marshalled his imagination to the cause of imaginative literature, he rendered unto art the things which are art's. But, when his mood altered a theme—switched an allegiance—he sold out his talent and his genius to the expediency of propaganda. No one has expressed so well the destructive ambivalence which in Wells produced a worship of false gods than Vincent Brome, his most recent biographer:

Wells had mistaken his vocation. By temperament an artist and by training a scientist, the conflict between the two remained to the end of his days, and it was inevitable that when the artist broke out of his real world into sociology he brought solutions which were intrinsically artistic. . . . They were highly subjective projections of Wells's own way of life, an attempt to make the cold, material outside world . . . susceptible to private ideals. . . . The artist broke into alien territory, and it was typical of the artist turned world-maker that he should brush aside enormous complications with a sweep of words only to leave them firmly in being. . . .[1]

T. S. Eliot put his finger directly on the divisiveness that has spoiled for future readers all but a handful of H. G. Wells's books. Wells's imagination was one thing, his ideas another.[2] The quality of the first was golden, of the second, metallic.

The demise of nearly all of Wells's fiction after *The Undying Fire* stands as eloquent testimony to his inability in his fiction to assert mind over imagination. It represented a change of stance in the interests of bolstering his public persona at the expense of his convictions. An aim of this study has been to show that the despair of *Mind at the End of Its Tether* was one fully anticipated in the introspective thrashings of his autobiography, a book which tells more by what it leaves unsaid than by what it says, and the scolding, often priggish, quality of the novels of his latter period. Wells returned at the end, a bitter old man, to the realities of the human situation. "He was by nature a pessimist," wrote his son, Anthony West; "and he was doing violence to his intuitions and his rational perceptions alike when he asserted in his middle period that mankind could make a better world for itself by an effort of will."[3]

Wells did violence to his reputation too. The falsely confident air of *The Outline of History*, as well as the mass of journalism and idea-novels peripheral to it, has had little appeal for intellectuals since the 1930's. It was, as Frederick J. Hoffman said, "too easy to believe."[4] Edmund Wilson told me that he once steered F. Scott Fitzgerald to Wells when both were Princeton undergraduates ("I did it to steer Scott's taste a notch higher than Booth Tarkington."); and that while he keeps a shelf of the Edwardians near his bed and is drawn frequently to Shaw and, most of all, to Beerbohm, he rarely takes up Wells.[5]

The Wells that holds up is the mythopoeic Wells of the scientific romances, which still stand, as science-fiction chroniclers Amis and Moskowitz proclaim,[6] supreme in their genre, and the intuitive sage of that comic Edwardian trio, Kipps, Polly, and Ponderevo.

The novels of society, except for the one—*The New Machiavelli* —that so impressed F. Scott Fitzgerald, are unreadable today. In their bold trumpetings for reform, however, they have enabled later novelists like D. H. Lawrence and E. M. Forster to turn their attention to more engrossing psychological aspects while taking for granted that Wells won the main engagements with the Edwardian Mrs. Grundys.

I cannot fully agree with that tireless researcher into Wells, Professor Robert P. Weeks, when he declares it probable that no responsible literary historian could be persuaded to reverse the verdict on Wells the novelist.[7] In Wells's period, his major novels represented an advance—yes, even in technique—over the excesses of the Victorians. Dickens's *Great Expectations* and *David Copperfield,* incomparably greater novels, are slower-going for the modern reader than *Kipps* and *Tono-Bungay*. Wells, who really belongs in the nineteenth century, lent pace to them.

Wells's gifts in the area of psychological probing were virtually non-existent. A novelist like Joyce Cary possesses as much vigor as Wells at his best and is capable of a gallery of characters denied his predecessor. It was inevitable that the Edwardian novel, predominantly realistic in tone, should utilize the rich materials offered by the rapidly changing social, industrial, and intellectual environment. Wells especially exploited the external world as it had been recreated by modern science. He, like Arnold Bennett and Galsworthy, but unlike James and Conrad, was concerned with the ethical and intellectual implications of the new order. The major Georgians have been interested, not in the superficial phenomena of Wells's catalyst, the Machine, but with exploring the psychological richness of the modern mind.

The stifling era that produced an H. G. Wells cannot be recreated. The grievances of Wells's student days have been mitigated. To the spiritually underfed youth of Post-Victorian days, H. G. Wells introduced a priceless ingredient: exhilaration. If Nihilist despair has temporarily superseded the anything-is-possible air of Wells's Darien, the best of H. G. Wells will not forever be denied.

Notes and References

Chapter One

1. H. G. Wells, *Experiment in Autobiography*, p. 83.
2. Van Wyck Brooks, *The World of H. G. Wells* (New York, 1915), p. 57.
3. *Experiment in Autobiography*, p. 37.
4. Brooks, *op. cit.*, 57.
5. *Experiment in Autobiography*, p. 83.
6. *Ibid.*, 106.
7. The manuscript of "The Desert Daisy," written sometime between 1878 and 1880, when Wells was twelve to fourteen, is now the property of the University of Illinois, which purchased the Wells Library and Papers in 1954. It was printed for the first time in 1957 with an introduction by Wells's official biographer, Gordon N. Ray (University of Illinois Press).
8. *Tono-Bungay*, from *The Works of H. G. Wells:* Atlantic Edition (28 vols. New York, 1924–27), XII, 63–65. All subsequent references to text in works of Wells to 1926 will be, where possible, to this definitive edition. Major exceptions will be in Chapter III ("The Scientific Romances") where references are to *Seven Famous Novels* (New York, 1934) and Chapter IV ("The Short Stories") where the omnibus *Famous Short Stories of H. G. Wells* (Garden City, 1938) is used.
9. Perhaps no other man of letters in this century has been accorded recognition of this kind. While a correspondent for the *London Tribune*, Wells lunched with President Theodore Roosevelt in 1906. He made his second journey to Russia in 1920 and spoke at length with Lenin. Wells returned to the Soviet Union in 1934, a few months after a visit to President Franklin D. Roosevelt. His interview with Stalin that year was widely publicized and set off a long debate with Bernard Shaw (see Vincent Brome, *Six Studies in Quarreling* [London, 1958] pp. 170–89). Wells addressed the German Reichstag on April 15, 1929, and the French Chamber heard him at about the same time.
10. *Experiment in Autobiography*, pp. 159–61.
11. Quoted in *Experiment in Autobiography*, p. 162.

12. Quoted in Mark R. Hillegas, "Cosmic Pessimism in H. G. Wells's Scientific Romances," *Papers of the Michigan Academy of Science, Arts, and Letters,* XLVI, 1961 (1960 Meeting), pp. 655–63.

13. *Ibid.,* p. 657.

14. Brooks, *op. cit.,* p. 48.

15. Anthony West, "The Dark World of H. G. Wells," *Harper's Magazine,* CCXIV (May, 1957), p. 68.

16. For a stimulating discussion of the man of science as protagonist in Wells's earliest scientific romances, see Bernard Bergonzi, *The Early H. G. Wells* (Toronto University, 1961), pp. 102–12.

Chapter Two

1. V. S. Pritchett, *The Living Novel* (New York, 1947), p. 122.

2. As far as I can learn, the remark was made in an interview in 1921. C. Hartley Grattan, "Good-Bye to H. G. Wells!", *Outlook and Independent,* CLVII (Feb. 4, 1931), p. 178, takes as ironic another quote by Anatole France—"Il [Wells] est le plus intelligent des Anglais!" However, Stanley Kauffmann, "Wells and the New Generation," *College English,* I (April, 1940), p. 574, quotes France as I have. There can be little doubt that the author of *Penguin Island* admired Wells. As noted by Joseph Conrad in a letter to Wells on Oct. 20, 1905, Anatole France wrote of Wells in *Sur la Pierre Blanche* (1905): "They are few who tried to penetrate the future from pure curiosity, without moral intention or an optimistic bias. I know only of H. G. Wells. . . ."

3. *Mr. Britling* earned Wells twenty thousand pounds in the United States alone (*Experiment in Autobiography,* p. 423).

4. For the most thorough and persuasive examination of the basic contradiction in Wells's mid-period, see Anthony West, "H. G. Wells," *Encounter,* VIII (February, 1957), pp. 52–59. It is also touched on by Pritchett, *op. cit.,* p. 127.

5. This is the definition of persona as Wells interprets it in Jung's use (*Experiment in Autobiography,* pp. 9–10).

6. See, among many tributes to Wells as a popularizer of science, Waldemar Kaempffert, "Evangelist of Utopia," *Saturday Review of Literature,* XXIX (Aug. 31, 1946), pp. 8–9.

7. Horace Gregory, "H. G. Wells: A Wreath for the Liberal Tradition," *New World Writing #11* (1957), p. 102.

8. One of the best studies of Wells's transcription of social, industrial, and intellectual life from 1900–1930 is contained in Fred B. Millett, *Contemporary British Literature* (New York, 1935), pp. 15–35.

9. George Orwell, "The True Pattern of H. G. Wells," *Manchester Evening News* (Aug. 14, 1946), p. 10.

10. Gerald Heard, "H. G. Wells: The End of a Faith," *Saturday Review of Literature,* XXXII (March 13, 1948), p. 9.

11. Odette Keun, "H. G. Wells—The Player," *Time and Tide,* XV (Oct. 27, 1934), p. 1347.

12. Heard, *op. cit.,* p. 9.

13. Wells, *The Outline of History,* III (New York, 1940–41), p. 1106.

14. Van Wyck Brooks, *Scenes and Portraits* (New York, 1954), p. 216.

15. West, "The Dark World," p. 68.

16. Hillegas, *op. cit.,* p. 655.

17. West, "The Dark World," 68.

18. Bertrand Russell, *Portraits from Memory* (New York, 1956), p. 75.

19. Kenneth Rexroth, "The Screw Turns on Mr. James," *Nation,* 187 (Aug. 16, 1958), pp. 76–77; Gregory, *op. cit.,* p. 109.

20. Mark Schorer, "Technique as Discovery," *Forms of Modern Fiction,* William Van O'Connor, ed. (University of Minnesota, 1948), p. 15.

Chapter Three

1. Godfrey Smith, in his profile of today's leading S.F. writer, cites Arthur Clarke's linking of *The Time Machine* and *Gulliver's Travels.* "Astounding Story! About a Science Fiction Writer!" *New York Times Magazine* (Mar. 6, 1966), p. 77.

2. Bergonzi, *op. cit.,* 43. There is an extended discussion of Wells's debt to Kipling in Ingvald Raknem, *H. G. Wells and His Critics* (New York, 1963), pp. 360–64.

3. A most articulate reaction against the linking of Verne and Wells comes from an unexpected source, the modern Argentinian writer, Jorge Luis Borges. See André Maurois, "A Note on Borges," *Paris Review #28* (Summer–Fall, 1962), pp. 118–19. Wells himself contrasts his work with that of Verne in *Seven Famous Novels,* introduction, pp. vii–viii.

4. Hillegas, "Cosmic Pessimism," p. 657.

5. Quoted by Hillegas, *ibid.,* p. 658.

6. Norman Nicholson, *H. G. Wells* (London, 1950), p. 28.

7. Pritchett, *op. cit.,* 125.

8. Winston Churchill, "H. G. Wells," London *Sunday Dispatch* (Aug. 26, 1946), p. 25.

9. Pritchett, *op. cit.,* 124.

10. The best account of the origins of *The Time Machine* is con-

tained in Bergonzi, pp. 25–38. His book also contains the text of *The Chronic Argonauts*, pp. 187–214.

11. Raknem, *op. cit.*, 15.

12. *Experiment in Autobiography*, p. 334.

13. London *Daily Chronicle* (July 27, 1895), p. 3.

14. See Mark R. Hillegas, "The Cosmic Voyage and the Doctrine of Inhabited Worlds in Nineteenth-Century English Literature," (unpublished dissertation, Columbia University, 1957), p. 199.

15. Carl Niemeyer, "The Coral Island Revisited," *College English*, XXII (January, 1961), pp. 241–45.

16. Leo J. Henkin, *Darwinism in the English Novel, 1860–1910* (New York, 1940), p. 193.

17. West, "The Dark World," p. 69.

18. Thomas H. Huxley, "Government: Anarchy or Regimentation," in *Method and Results—Essays* (New York, 1894), p. 423.

19. Chalmers Mitchell, (a review) *The Saturday Review,* LXXXII (Nov. 7, 1896), p. 498.

20. Wells, *Seven Famous Novels* (New York, 1934), p. ix.

21. Charles Darwin, *The Origin of Species* (New York, n.d.), p. 474. Also quoted in Henkin, *op. cit.*, p. 197.

22. H. G. Wells, *Mind at the End of Its Tether* (New York, 1946), p. 17.

23. Dashiell Hammett, *Creeps by Night* (New York, 1944), introduction, n.p.

24. Nicholson, *op. cit.*, p. 35.

25. Brooks, *The World of H. G. Wells*, pp. 27–29.

26. Hadley Cantril, *The Invasion from Mars* (Princeton University, 1940), p. 16. Howard Koch wrote the scenario.

27. Bergonzi, *op. cit.*, p. 133.

28. For a good discussion of the relationship of *The War of the Worlds* to scientific suggestions and discoveries of the late nineteenth century, see Raknem, *op. cit.*, pp. 400–03; Mark R. Hillegas, "The First Invasions from Mars," *Michigan Alumnus Quarterly Review,* LXVI (Winter, 1960), pp. 107–12; Hillegas, "The Cosmic Voyage," pp. 139–49; and David Hughes, "An Edition and a Survey of H. G. Wells's *The War of the Worlds*" (unpublished dissertation, University of Illinois, 1962).

29. There is an exceptionally lucid, although clearly unsympathetic portrayal of Wells's struggle to gain acceptance of the literati during the Edwardian era in Leon Edel and Gordon N. Ray, eds., *Henry James and H. G. Wells* (U. of Illinois, 1958), pp. 15–41.

30. Royal Gettmann, *George Gissing and H. G. Wells* (University of Illinois, 1961), p. 25.

31. Hillegas, "The Cosmic Voyage," pp. 213–14.

32. Quoted in London *Sunday Times,* Jan. 19, 1964 ("Wells's Son Treads the Path of the Moon Men"), unsigned, p. 33.

33. Hillegas, "The Cosmic Voyage," p. 219.

34. Harris Wilson, ed., *Arnold Bennett* and *H. G. Wells* (University of Illinois, 1960), pp. 260–65.

35. "Jules Verne Revisited," *T. P.'s Weekly* (Oct. 9, 1903), p. 589. Also quoted in Bergonzi, *op. cit.,* pp. 157–58.

36. Wells, *Seven Famous Novels,* p. vii.

37. "The Unparalleled Adventure of One Hans Pfaal" (1835) is not one of Poe's best stories, but it moves the literature of the cosmic voyage ahead. During his balloon journey Pfaal kept a log which included comments on the gravitational effects between moon and earth.

38. See Hillegas, "Cosmic Pessimism," p. 662n.

39. See Edgar Johnson, *A Treasury of Satire* (New York, 1945), p. 576. Also Pritchett, *op. cit.,* pp. 123–24. Wells's own tributes to Swift are too numerous to mention.

Chapter Four

1. H. E. Bates, *The Modern Short Story* (Boston, 1941), pp. 110–11.

2. This is not to suggest that Conrad Aiken's "Mr. Arcularis" derived from Wells's "Under the Knife." It is true, however, that both stories revolve around the dreams of men under surgery. "Mr. Arcularis," published in 1931 and endlessly anthologized, is a modern classic. "Under the Knife," published in 1896, was once referred to by Joseph Conrad in a letter to Wells as establishing its author as a poet.

3. Frank Swinnerton, *Swinnerton: An Autobiography* (London, 1937), p. 197.

4. *Experiment in Autobiography,* p. 428.

5. Raknem, *op. cit.,* p. 347.

6. Pritchett is most expansive on this point, *op. cit.,* p. 123.

7. Raknem, *op. cit.,* p. 341.

8. H. G. Wells, "The Lord of the Dynamos," in *The Famous Short Stories of H. G. Wells* (Garden City, 1938), p. 277. All references to text of Wells's short stories are to this edition.

9. Thomas H. Huxley, *Evolution and Ethics and Other Essays* (New York, 1904), pp. 16–17.

10. I could find no evidence that Eugene O'Neill had read "The Lord of the Dynamos." However, both Yank in *The Hairy Ape* and Azuma-zi in the Wells story are symbolic of man who has lost his old harmony with nature. Yank worships the engines of the ship because they appear to give him, a stoker, a sense of "belonging." Azuma-zi sees the dynamo as an extension of his heathen idols.

11. Bergonzi, *op. cit.*, 70–71. Quoted in George Hichfield, *Henry Adams: An Introduction and Interpretation* (New York, 1962), p. 118.

12. Bergonzi, *op. cit.*, p. 19.

13. See Lewis Mumford, "The Revolt of the Demons," *The New Yorker* (May 23, 1964), p. 171.

14. The Wells Archive, University of Illinois, contains the letter of rejection.

15. W. Warren Wagar, *H. G. Wells and the World State* (Yale, 1961), p. 239 n.

16. *Experiment in Autobiography*, pp. 389–91.

17. *Bennett and Wells, op. cit.*, p. 59.

18. Reginald Pound, *Arnold Bennett, a Biography* (London, 1952), p. 114.

19. Bergonzi, *op. cit.*, p. 88.

20. H. G. Wells, *The Country of the Blind* (London, 1939), pp. 7–8. The Wells Archives, University of Illinois, contains one of 280 numbered copies of this rare edition containing two versions of Wells's most famous short story.

21. Bergonzi, *op. cit.*, p. 81.

22. Maugham, *op. cit.*, pp. 218–28.

23. Wells, *End of Tether*, p. 17.

Chapter Five

1. Winston Churchill, *op. cit.*, p. 25, wrote that H. G. Wells nursed a grievance against the British Empire, the United Kingdom, and, in particular, against England, which, like an "uncomfortable and querulous baby . . . he has to carry with him everywhere." Richard Rees, in *George Orwell: Fugitive from the Camp of Victory* (London, 1961) is especially interesting on Wells as an angry young man, pp. 18–19, 130–31.

2. Wells, *Works*, XVII, p. 212.

3. E. M. Forster, *Aspects of the Novel* (New York, 1927), pp. 110–11.

4. *Experiment in Autobiography*, p. 20.

5. Nicholson, *op. cit.*, p. 55.

6. Wells, *Works*, V, p. ix.

7. Raknem, *op. cit.*, p. 76.

8. *Ibid.*, 69.

9. C. E. M. Joad, "The Most Ordinary of Great Men," London *Evening Standard* (Aug. 14, 1946), p. 6.

10. Vincent Brome, *H. G. Wells* (London and New York, 1951), p. 110.

11. Sinclair Lewis, Foreword, *The History of Mr. Polly* (New York, 1941), p. vii.

12. Sidney Dark, *Outline of Wells* (New York, 1922), p. 121.

Chapter Six

1. For the analogy between Wells and Shaw I am indebted to Clifton Fadiman, "The Passing of a Prophet," *Saturday Review of Literature* XXIX (Aug. 31, 1946), p. 4. In his Preface to *Man and Superman* Shaw extols the idea of "being used for a purpose recognized by yourself as a mighty one . . . [of] being a force of Nature instead of a feverish little clod of ailments and grievances complaining that the world will not devote itself to making you happy. . . ."

2. Grattan, *op. cit.*, p. 178.

3. Wells, *Works*, VI, pp. 313–18.

4. It is interesting to note that in one of his last articles Wells dwells ironically on "the collapse of an inflated reputation," putting the words in the pen of one Wilfred B. Betterave. Writing "at the suggestion of H. G. Wells himself," Betterave calls the essay " 'All's Well That Ends Wells', a complete exposé of this notorious literary humbug." In the course of his satire Wells has Betterave accuse Wells of inventing the tank in "The Land Ironclads" in 1903—"an impudent plagiarism of Sir Ernest Swinton's inspiration in 1914 (whereby) *Wells merely plagiarized the idea beforehand instead of afterwards.*" See Wells, "The Betterave Papers," *The Virginia Quarterly Review*, p. xxi (Summer, 1945), pp. 420–33.

5. See Edward R. Pease, *The History of the Fabian Society* (New York, 1916), Chapter IX, "The Episode of Mr. Wells." Other tributes to Wells's Fabian tracts in Margaret Cole, *The Story of Fabian Socialism* (Stanford University, 1961), p. 119, and A. M. McBriar, *Fabian Socialism and English Politics 1884–1918* (London, 1962), p. 185.

6. George Bernard Shaw, "The Man I Knew," *The New Statesman and Nation* (Aug. 17, 1946), p. 115.

7. *Experiment in Autobiography*, p. 566.

8. Leonard Woolf, "Some Portraits," *Encounter*, XXII (May, 1964), p. 80. Woolf credits A. L. Rowse for the words.

9. Wells, *Works*, IX, p. 379.

10. *Ibid.*, I, p. xi.

11. See William C. Frierson, *The English Novel in Transition* (University of Oklahoma, 1942), pp. 131–35.

12. Geoffrey West, *H. G. Wells: A Sketch for a Portrait* (New York, 1930), p. 237.

13. H. G. Wells, *The First Men in the Moon*, in *Seven Famous Novels*, p. 416.

14. Wells was a connoisseur of outsiders, writes John Raymond, "Alive and Kicking," *New Statesman* (Jan. 10, 1959), p. 46, an acute paralleling of the roles of Wells and Lloyd George. Wells always thought adventurous outsiders are inevitable in periods of obsolete educational ideas and decaying social conditions. He included himself as one. *Experiment in Autobiography*, p. 439.

15. Harry T. Moore, Foreword, *Tono-Bungay* (Signet Classics, 1960), p. xii.

16. See especially Antonina Vallentin, *H. G. Wells: Prophet of Our Day* (New York, 1950), p. 156.

17. *Experiment in Autobiography*, p. 493.

Chapter Seven

1. *Experiment in Autobiography*, p. 661.
2. Raknem, *op. cit.*, p. 95.
3. Wells, *Works*, XIV, p. ix.
4. John Raymond, *loc. cit.*, is amusing on this point. He describes Wells's picture of the Webbs as "unfair and unflattering" and reproduces as true this exchange between the couple when they read *The New Machiavelli:* "I'm in it," said Beatrice Webb cheerfully to Desmond MacCarthy. "I'm the woman whose voice is described as a 'strangulated contralto'. . . . But you are not, Sydney." . . . "Oh, yes, I am. I'm described as 'one of those supplementary males often found among the lower crustaceans'." "Alive and Kicking," *New Statesman* (Jan. 10, 1959), p. 46.
5. Anthony West quoted, "The Dark World," p. 68.
6. Raknem, *op. cit.*, p. 116.
7. Pound, *op. cit.*, p. 262.
8. André Maurois, *Prophets and Poets* (New York, 1935), p. 87.
9. Raknem, *op. cit.*, p. 104.
10. *Experiment in Autobiography*, p. 297.
11. Montgomery Belgion, *H. G. Wells* (London, 1953), p. 23.
12. For fairly obvious reasons Wells's amatory and polygamous tendencies have been barely touched on in my study. Three revealing accounts are contained in Maugham, *op. cit.*, pp. 220–21; Sir Arthur Salter, *Personality in Politics* (London, 1947), p. 134; Rexroth, *op. cit.*, pp. 76–77.
13. Rexroth, *op. cit.*, p. 76.
14. Brome, *op. cit.*, p. 112.
15. Wells expresses his debt to the liberating spirit of Shelley's poems throughout his autobiography and in many of his novels. Edmund Wilson expressed to me the view that the influence of Wells and Shaw on his generation may have been, in the final analysis, damaging:

Notes and References

"They were too Rousseavian—Wells and Shaw—and their novels and plays never go on to trace the outcome of the polygamous situations they herald. Many men and women of my generation saw in these books carte blanche for complete permissiveness and were irreparably injured."

16. *Experiment in Autobiography,* p. 147.
17. Brome, *op. cit.,* p. 110.
18. Wells, *Works,* XIII, p. 11.
19. Keun, *op. cit.,* p. 1307.
20. Wells, *Works,* XIII, p. ix.
21. Doris J. Schwalbe, "H. G. Wells and the Superfluous Woman," (unpublished dissertation, University of Colorado, 1962), p. 14.
22. *Ibid.,* pp. 58–59.
23. Quoted in Brome, *op. cit.,* p. 112.
24. *Ibid.*
25. Edwin E. Slosson, *Six Major Prophets* (Boston, 1917), p. 113.
26. Nicholson, *op. cit.,* p. 72.
27. Edmund Wilson, "T. S. Eliot and the Church of England," in *A Literary Chronicle: 1920–1950* (Garden City, 1956), p. 135.
28. See Brome, *op. cit.,* pp. 196–97, 198, 199, 201.
29. Schwalbe, *op. cit.,* p. 45.

Chapter Eight

1. Virginia Woolf, "Mr. Bennett and Mrs. Brown," in Clifton Fadiman, *Reading I've Liked* (New York, 1941), pp. 361–79. Essay was originally read before the Heretics Club at Cambridge, May 18, 1924.
2. J. I. M. Stewart, *Eight Modern Writers,* (London, 1963), p. 11.
3. Stanley Kauffmann, "Wells and the New Generation: The Decline of a Leader of Youth," *College English,* I (April, 1940), p. 574.
4. Wells, *Works,* XXVII, p. ix.
5. *Experiment in Autobiography,* p. 614.
6. Wells, *Works,* VII, p. ix.
7. *Henry James and H. G. Wells,* eds. Leon Edel and Gordon N. Ray (University of Illinois, 1958), p. 67.
8. *Ibid.,* p. 16.
9. Dorothy Richardson, *The Tunnel* (Vol. II of *Pilgrimage*), New York, 1947), especially pp. 109–43.
10. *James and Wells,* p. 27.
11. Michael Swan, "Henry James and H. G. Wells: A Study of Their Friendship Based on Their Unpublished Correspondence," *The Cornhill,* CMXCVII (Autumn, 1953), p. 43.
12. *James and Wells,* p. 105.
13. *Ibid.,* p. 123.

14. *Ibid.*, p. 128.

15. *Ibid.*, p. 168.

16. *Ibid.*, p. 27.

17. Wells gives an interesting account of popular taste in the Edwardian days in a preface to an omnibus volume, *Stories of Men and Women in Love* (London, 1933), containing *Love and Mr. Lewisham, Secret Places of the Heart, The Passionate Friends,* and *The Wife of Sir Isaac Harman.*

18. Wells, *Works,* IX, pp. 379–80.

19. *James and Wells,* p. 32.

20. Henry James, "The New Novel," in *Notes on Novelists, with Some Other Notes* (New York, 1914), p. 319.

21. *Ibid.*, p. 334.

22. *James and Wells,* p. 266.

23. *Ibid.*, p. 267.

24. *Ibid.*, p. 267 n.

25. Wells's letter to Joyce, dated Nov. 23, 1928, is reprinted in *The Atlantic Monthly,* CXCIX (April, 1957), p. 62 ("The Writing of *Ulysses,* Letters of James Joyce," ed. by Stuart Gilbert). However, it should be noted that Wells elsewhere has expressed his deep admiration for the works of Joyce (see especially his essay on *A Portrait of the Artist as a Young Man* in *Novelists on Novelists,* ed. by Louis Kronenberger (Garden City, 1962), pp. 343–46.

26. *James and Wells,* p. 264.

27. Sidney Dark, *op. cit.*, p. 98.

28. Nicholson, *op. cit.*, p. 82.

29. Quoted in Edmund Wilson, *op. cit.*, p. 135.

30. *Experiment in Autobiography,* p. 575.

31. Brome, *op. cit.*, pp. 232–33.

32. Rebecca West, (a review), *The New Republic* (Nov. 20, 1915), p. 4.

33. Quoted by Edward Mead Earle, "H. G. Wells, British Patriot in Search of a World State," *Nationalism and Internationalism* (Columbia University, 1950), p. 84.

34. In conversation, July 23, 1963.

35. Keun, *op. cit.*, pp. 1346–47.

36. Quoted by Salter, *op. cit.*, p. 120.

Chapter Nine

1. This is not to suggest that either Aldous Huxley or Zamiatin merits the distinction. *Brave New World* (1932) certainly was an effective rebuttal to Wells's *Men Like Gods* (1923) and a work which

is imprinted in the popular mind as the first book which looked at the future of civilization darkly. However, as George Orwell has pointed out, Huxley owes a great deal to Wells's *The Sleeper Awakes*. He also finds *Brave New World* derives partly from a book by a Russian, Eugene Zamiatin, which he (Orwell) read in a French translation, *Nous Autres*. Writing in 1946, Orwell noted that both the Huxley novel and the one written in 1923 by Zamiatin deal with the rebellion of the primitive human spirit against a rationalized, mechanized, painless world and both are supposed to take place six hundred years hence. Orwell's tribute to Zamiatin and his dystopian work—English title, *We*—is well worth reading (Orwell, "Freedom and Happiness," London *Tribune*, Jan. 4, 1946, p. 15). Orwell's own *1984* also bears the unmistakable influence of *We*. I could find no evidence to substantiate my belief that Zamiatin was deeply influenced by *The Sleeper Awakes*. However, Zamiatin was the first editor of a Russian edition of Wells in the U.S.S.R. Dutton published a U.S. edition of *The Sleeper* in 1952 and a paperback edition in 1960.

2. Anthony West, "H. G. Wells," *Encounter* 8 (1957), p. 55.

3. See Sylvia E. Bowman *et al.*, *Edward Bellamy Abroad*, (New York, 1962), p. 116.

4. Orwell, "The True Pattern," p. 10.

5. See *Writers at Work: 'Paris Review' Interviews* (2nd Series), (New York, 1963), p. 198.

6. E. F. Bleiler, Introduction, *Three Science-Fiction Novels of H. G. Wells* (Dover Edition, 1960), pp. ix–x.

7. Bernard Shaw, *Man and Superman*, Act II (New York, 1962) III, pp. 564–65.

8. Frank Swinnerton, *Swinnerton: An Autobiography*, (London, 1937), p. 198.

9. J. G. Riewald, ed., *Max in Verse* (Brattleboro, Vt., 1963), p. 54.

10. Nicholson, *op. cit.*, p. 37.

11. Wells, *Works*, IX, p. 20.

12. Slosson, *op. cit.*, p. 101.

13. Maugham, *op. cit.*, p. 225.

14. Maurois, *op. cit.*, p. 92.

15. Wells, *Works*, XI, p. xi.

16. Vallentin, *op. cit.*, p. 236.

17. *Ibid.*, pp. 236–37.

18. Wagar, *op. cit.*, p. 252.

19. *Writers at Work*, p. 198.

20. West, "The Dark World," p. 73.

21. *Ibid.*

22. Wells, *World Brain* (Garden City, 1938), p. 134.

23. Carl L. Becker, "Mr. Wells and the New History," in *Everyman His Own Historian* (New York, 1930), p. 190.

24. Wagar, *op. cit.*, 139 n.

25. *Experiment in Autobiography*, p. 613.

26. Becker, *op. cit.*, p. 187.

27. *Ibid.*, p. 185.

28. Wells, *The World of William Clissold*, I (New York, 1926), pp. 80–81.

29. Becker, *op. cit.*, p. 171.

30. Wells, *The Outline of History*, I (New York, 1940), p. 81.

31. Golding quotes the offending section of *The Outline* on the flyleaf of *The Inheritors*.

32. Henkin, *op. cit.*, p. 193.

33. Wagar, *op. cit.*, p. 146.

34. Quoted in Wagar, p. 146.

35. *Ibid.*, p. 145.

36. *Experiment in Autobiography*, p. 615.

37. Aldous Huxley, *The Olive Tree* (New York, 1937), pp. 14–15.

38. Quoted in Wagar, *op. cit.*, p. 147.

39. *Ibid.*

40. Wells, *Outline of History*, III, pp. 1195–97.

41. Wells, *Mind at the End of Its Tether*, p. 30.

42. Maugham, *op. cit.*, p. 223. Mr. Maugham himself repeated this story when I interviewed him at his villa at St. Jean-Cap Ferrat, Sept. 9, 1959. See R. H. Costa, "An Interview with Maugham," *The National Observer* (Apr. 15, 1962), p. 4.

Chapter Ten

1. Wells, *Work, Wealth and Happiness of Mankind* (New York, 1932), p. 21.

2. Salter, *op. cit.*, 124.

3. Colin Wilson, *The Strength to Dream* (Boston, 1962), p. 107.

4. Nicholson, *op. cit.*, p. 86.

5. See Lawrence's review of *Clissold* in *Phoenix: The Posthumous Papers of D. H. Lawrence*, ed., Edward D. McDonald (New York, 1936), pp. 349–50.

6. "The Man I Knew," *op. cit.*, p. 115.

7. Wells, *Clissold*, I, pp. 29–30.

8. Wells, *Apropos of Dolores* (New York, 1938), p. 1.

9. Wells, *Brynhild* (New York, 1937), pp. 1–2.

10. *Experiment in Autobiography*, p. 1.

11. *Ibid.*, p. 6.

12. West, "H. G. Wells," *op. cit.*, p. 53.
13. H. L. Mencken, *Prejudices: First Series* (New York, 1919), pp. 22–23.
14. The letter, dated Oct. 3, 1928, is among those in the Wells Archive, University of Illinois, Urbana, Ill.
15. *Experiment in Autobiography*, p. 665.
16. *Ibid.*, p. 69.
17. See "H. G. Wells-Joseph Stalin," in *The Book of Great Conversations*, ed., Louis Biancolli (New York, 1948), pp. 559–60.
18. *Experiment in Autobiography*, p. 697.
19. See George Catlin, "Prophet of Modernism," *The Commonweal* (Sept. 27, 1946), p. 573.
20. Wells, *World Brain*, p. 35.
21. Vallentin, *op. cit.*, p. 297.
22. F. T. Marsh, (a review) *Books* (Oct. 6, 1940), p. 4.
23. Letter, contained in Wells Archive, was written Aug. 24, 1932, as part of a criticism of Swinnerton's novel of that year, *The Georgian House*. Wells wrote: ". . . But I maintain an artificial story is a perfectly justifiable way of holding together a bunch of people if their reactions are real and living."
24. H. G. Wells, *Babes in the Darkling Wood* (New York, 1940), p. 39.
25. Vallentin, *op. cit.*, p. 308.
26. Anecdote told by Miss Bowen at a lecture at the Art Alliance in Philadelphia, Pa., the night of Nov. 10, 1958.
27. Colin Wilson, *The Outsider* (Boston, 1956), p. 18.
28. Wells, *Mind at The End of its Tether*, p. 17.
29. *Ibid.*, p. 2.
30. *Ibid.*
31. Weeks, *op. cit.*, p. 15.

Chapter Eleven

1. Brome, *op. cit.*, pp. 237–38.
2. T. S. Eliot, "Rudyard Kipling," in *On Poetry and Poets*, (New York, 1957), p. 289.
3. West, "H. G. Wells," *op. cit.*, p. 53.
4. Frederick J. Hoffman, *The Twenties* (New York, 1948), p. 345.
5. Edmund Wilson discussed Wells with me on a number of occasions, dating from the summer of 1963. He acknowledged Wells's influence on his (Wilson's) generation as "tremendous, just tremendous." He said he had read all of the scientific romances, the short stories collected under the title of *Twelve Stories and a Dream*, and most of the novels through *The Autocracy of Mr. Parham* (1930). Of the

scientific romances, he particularly liked *The Island of Dr. Moreau*. He quoted from memory and with evident relish the last lines of "A Dream of Armageddon": "Nightmares . . . nightmares, indeed! My God! Great birds that fought and tore."

6. Sam Moskowitz, *Explorers of the Infinite: Shapers of Science Fiction* (New York, 1963), p. 53. Reference has already been made to Amis's tribute in his *New Maps of Hell*.

7. Robert P. Weeks, "Wells Scholarship in Perspective," *English Fiction in Transition* III, 1 (Purdue University, 1960), p. 15.

Selected Bibliography

PRIMARY SOURCES

The most important collection of Wells papers is now the Wells Archive at the University of Illinois. For the purposes of this critical study the materials, while not nearly so valuable as Wells's published writings, often yielded a strikingly valuable letter, or a press clipping, or an entry from an appointment book to buttress an insight. The Archive contains several thousand letters whose range of correspondents is perhaps more impressive than the letters themselves. On vital points the letters contain little that Wells did not say in print.

The following bibliography lists chronologically only the major publications, and only the fiction titles are complete. For a listing of Wells's enormous output of journalism, see W. Warren Wagar's *H. G. Wells and the World State* (New Haven: Yale University Press, 1961). The only important collected edition of Wells's writings is *The Works of H. G. Wells*: Atlantic Edition (28 vols. London: Unwin; and New York: Scribner's, 1924–27), prepared by Wells himself. For students of Wells the principal service of the Edition is the preface Wells wrote for each volume. *Seven Famous Novels by H. G. Wells* (New York: Knopf, 1934), with a revealing preface by the author, and *The Famous Short Stories of H. G. Wells* (Garden City: Doubleday, 1938) are easily the best among numerous omnibus science-fiction and short-story compilations. Both are used for text references in this book.

The Time Machine. New York: Holt & Company, 1895.
The Stolen Bacillus and Other Incidents. London: Macmillan, 1895.
The Wonderful Visit. New York: Macmillan, 1895.
The Island of Dr. Moreau. New York: Stone & Kimball, 1896.
The Wheels of Chance. New York: Macmillan, 1896.
The Plattner Story and Others. London: Macmillan, 1897.
The Invisible Man. New York: Harper, 1897.
Thirty Strange Stories. New York: Harper, 1897.
The War of the Worlds. London: Heinemann, 1898.
When the Sleeper Wakes. London: Nelson, 1899. Republished, 1910

and 1911, by Nelson, in a revised and altered edition, entitled *The Sleeper Awakes.*

Tales of Space and Time. New York: Doubleday & McClure, 1899.

Love and Mr. Lewisham. London: Harper, 1900.

Anticipations of the Reaction of Mechanical and Scientific Progress Upon Human Life and Thought. London: Chapman & Hall, 1901.

The First Men in the Moon. Indianapolis: Bowen-Merrill, 1901.

The Sea Lady. New York: D. Appleton & Company, 1902.

Mankind in the Making. London: Chapman & Hall, 1903.

Twelve Stories and a Dream. London: Macmillan, 1903.

The Food of the Gods. New York: Scribner's, 1904.

A Modern Utopia. New York: Scribner's, 1905.

Kipps. New York: Scribner's, 1905.

In the Days of the Comet. New York: The Century Company, 1906.

First and Last Things. London: Constable, 1908.

New Worlds for Old. New York: Macmillan, 1908.

The War in the Air. New York: Macmillan, 1908.

Tono-Bungay. New York: Duffield, 1909.

Ann Veronica. New York: Harper, 1909.

The History of Mr. Polly. New York: Duffield, 1910.

The New Machiavelli. New York: Duffield, 1910.

The Country of the Blind and Other Stories. London: Nelson, 1911.

The Door in the Wall and Other Stories. New York: Mitchell Kennerley, 1911.

Marriage. New York: Duffield, 1912.

The Passionate Friends. New York: Harper, 1913.

The World Set Free. New York: Dutton, 1914.

The War That Will End War. New York: Duffield, 1914.

The Wife of Sir Isaac Harman. New York: Macmillan, 1914.

Bealby. New York: Macmillan, 1915.

Boon. New York: Doran, 1915.

The Research Magnificent. New York: Macmillan, 1915.

Mr. Britling Sees It Through. New York: Macmillan, 1916.

God the Invisible King. New York: Macmillan, 1917.

The Soul of a Bishop. New York: Macmillan, 1917.

Joan and Peter. New York: Macmillan, 1918.

The Undying Fire. New York: Macmillan, 1919.

The Outline of History. New York: Macmillan, 1920.

Russia in the Shadows. New York: Doran, 1921.

The Salvaging of Civilization. New York: Macmillan, 1921.

The Secret Places of the Heart. New York: Macmillan, 1922.

Men Like Gods. New York: Macmillan, 1923.

The Story of a Great Schoolmaster. New York: Macmillan, 1924.

Selected Bibliography

The Dream. New York: Macmillan, 1924.

Christina Alberta's Father. New York: Macmillan, 1925.

The World of William Clissold. New York: Doran, 1926.

Meanwhile. New York: Doran, 1927.

Mr. Blettsworthy on Rampole Island. New York: Doran, 1928.

The Open Conspiracy: Blue Prints for a World Revolution. New York: Doubleday, Doran, 1928.

The Autocracy of Mr. Parham. New York: Doran, 1930.

The Science of Life (with Julan Huxley and G. P. Wells), New York: Doubleday, Doran, 1931.

The Work, Wealth and Happiness of Mankind. New York: Doubleday, Doran, 1932.

The Shape of Things to Come. New York: Macmillan, 1933.

The Bulpington of Blup. New York: Macmillan, 1933.

Experiment in Autobiography: Discoveries and Conclusions of a Very Ordinary Brain (Since 1866). New York: Macmillan, 1934.

The Anatomy of Frustration. New York: Macmillan, 1936.

The Croquet Player. New York: Macmillan, 1937.

Brynhild. New York: Scribner's, 1937.

Apropos of Dolores. New York: Scribner's, 1938.

World Brain. New York: Doubleday, Doran, 1938.

The Brothers. New York: Viking, 1938.

The Holy Terror. New York: Simon & Schuster, 1939.

The Fate of Man. New York: Alliance, 1939.

Babes in the Darkling Wood. New York: Alliance, 1940.

All Aboard for Ararat. New York: Alliance, 1941.

You Can't Be Too Careful. New York: Alliance, 1942.

'42 to '44. New York: Alliance, 1944.

Mind at the End of Its Tether and *The Happy Turning.* New York: Didier, 1946.

SECONDARY SOURCES

1. Bibliographical Materials

Chappell, Fred A. *Bibliography of H. G. Wells.* Chicago: Covici-Mc-Gee, 1924. A chronological listing, fairly complete, of the published works from 1892–1924. For the present scholar, the bibliography of primary sources is valuable for its accurate chronology. The section called "Wellsiana"—the critical studies on Wells—is necessarily outdated.

Raknem, Ingvald. *H. G. Wells and His Critics.* New York: Hillary House, 1963. An incredibly detailed and chaotic work of scholarship; upwards of 150,000 words spun out of other people's opinions, 1,700 footnotes, forty-five pages of lists of books and book reviews and, unfortunately, no index. Nothing comparable has been done on H. G. Wells in forty years. The chief value of this book lies in its well-documented narrative of changes in critical attitudes through the years. Dr. Raknem, a Norwegian, has an easy style but devotes himself to laboring the obvious when he gives pages over to the task of proving Wells was almost wholly an autobiographical writer.

Wells, Geoffrey H. *The Works of H. G. Wells 1887–1925: A Bibliography, Dictionary and Subject-Index*. London: Routledge & Sons, 1926. This exhaustive, useful book by the man who in 1930, under the pseudonym Geoffrey West, wrote the best biography of Wells, will probably never be preempted. Encyclopedic in scope, no Wells scholar should be without it.

2. Biographies

No definitive biography of Wells has been written; two, either or both of which might fill the gap, have been promised. Anthony West, the novelist and critic, first announced he was working on the "authorized" biography of his father fifteen years ago. Gordon N. Ray, now of the Guggenheim Foundation, reported shortly after bringing the Wells Archive to the University of Illinois in 1954 that he was at work on the biography. Many persons who figured prominently in personal aspects of Wells's life are still alive. It may be years before a definitive biography can be published.

Brome, Vincent. *H. G. Wells*. London, New York and Toronto: Longmans, Green and Co., 1951. A highly readable, non-scholarly work whose final chapter is a brilliant exposition of the schizoid tendencies in Wells. The book, however, is too full of evasions and palpable reconstructions of the truth for the air of authenticity necessary to the authoritative biography.

Vallentin, Antonina. *H. G. Wells: Prophet of Our Day*. Translated by Daphne Woodward. New York: John Day, 1950. Only slightly above the level of woman's-magazine journalism, Madame Vallentin's paste-up album rarely succeeds even on its own terms. There are too many living figures standing between the author and the romantic and scandalous story she would prefer to tell.

West, Geoffrey (pseudonym of Geoffrey H. Wells). *H. G. Wells: A Sketch for a Portrait*. New York: W. W. Norton & Co., 1930. Still the best biography. The author, who knew Wells intimately during his heyday, gives a glowing yet fair estimate of Wells as a creative artist. Its early publication was saved the fading promises of Wells's last two decades. Chapter 13, "A Personal Interpretation," is in my view the finest literary essay ever written on Wells.

3. Critical Studies

The following list makes no pretense of being anything but fragmentary. I have emphasized general studies rather than appraisals of individual works. I have selected those studies which shed the brightest light on Wells from present vantage rather than those whose perspective was merely post-Victorian, Edwardian, or any other limited phase in time and place. Other sources are listed in Notes and References.

Amis, Kingsley. *New Maps of Hell: A Survey of Science Fiction.* New York: Harcourt, Brace & Co., 1960. Notable for its forecast that "Wells will soon get all, instead of part, of the recognition as pioneer [of science fiction] he clearly deserves."

Bates, H. E. *The Modern Short Story.* Boston: The Writer, Inc., 1941. A modern short-story master accords high rank to Wells in the genre while supplying an effective rebuttal to charges that Wells's style lacked beauty.

Becker, Carl L., *Everyman His Own Historian.* New York: F. S. Crofts & Co., 1935. The essay, "Mr. Wells and the New History," (pp. 169–90) not only stands as one of the best critiques of Wells as a historian but as a thinker.

Belgion, Montgomery. *H. G. Wells.* Published for the British Council and National Book League. London: Longmans, Green and Co., 1953. Belgion pinpoints Wells's major limitation as a novelist: the fact that all his major characters were his own alter-egos.

Bergonzi, Bernard. *The Early H. G. Wells: A Study of the Scientific Romances.* Toronto: University of Toronto, 1961. The definitive study of Wells as minor myth-maker and *fin-de-siècle* spokesman. Mr. Bergonzi is occasionally given to imposing Freudian-Jungian-Nietzschean analyses on the scientific romances and short stories.

Borges, Jorge Luis. "The First Wells." *Other Inquisitions, 1937–52.* Austin: University of Texas Press, 1964. This short essay (pp. 86–9) contains the epigraph to this book. In paying tribute to Wells's early scientific romances, Borges finds in them, not only an ingenious story, but tales "symbolic of processes somehow inherent in all human destinies."

Brooks, Van Wyck. *The World of H. G. Wells.* New York: Mitchell Kennerley, 1915. The earliest book-length critical study of Wells. Although Brooks in his latter years never listed it, the study is perceptive for its time and supplies an ironic commentary on the path a leading disciple saw ahead for a Wells who had not the stomach to follow it.

Caudwell, Christopher. *Studies in a Dying Culture*. London: The Bodley Head, 1938. "H. G. Wells: A Study in Utopianism" (pp. 73–95) could be taken as an elaboration on Trotsky's allegation that Lenin thought Wells hopelessly bourgeois. An effective Marxist polemic.

Earle, Edward Mead, "H. G. Wells, British Patriot in Search of a World State." *Nationalism and Internationalism*. Edited by Edward Mead Earle. New York: Columbia University, 1950 (pp. 79–121). Prof. Earle clearly has had to read every line of Wells's journalism to assemble so clear an analysis of the ideas of Wells.

Edel, Leon and Gordon N. Ray, eds. *Henry James and H. G. Wells*. Urbana: University of Illinois, 1958. A clear picture of external aspects of the James-Wells friendship and falling out.

Forster, E. M. *Aspects of the Novel*. New York: Harcourt, Brace & Co., 1927. Notable in its sympathy for Wells in his dispute with James. Also contains perhaps the best capsule likeness between the styles of Dickens and Wells.

Frierson, William C. *The English Novel in Transition*. Norman: University of Oklahoma, 1942. An attempt to place Wells in the mainstream of the "Life Novel"—the novel, like *Jean Christophe*, which is a portrait of an entire generation.

Grattan, C. Hartley. "Good-Bye to H. G. Wells!", *Outlook*, CLVII (February 4, 1931), 178–79. An unsympathetic view, mercilessly perceptive, of the qualities in Wells's thinking that lost him his audience in the last twenty years of his life.

Gregory, Horace, "H. G. Wells: A Wreath for the Liberal Tradition," *New World Writing #11*, 1957. Wells has always fared well at the hands of poets as tributes from Eliot, Spender, and Yevtushenko show. Gregory, a poet, finds that Wells still "haunts our feelings and certain sections of our minds."

Heard, Gerald, "H. G. Wells: The End of a Faith," *The Saturday Review of Literature* XXXII (March 13, 1948), 9–10. The death of Wells marked the end of Utopianism, writes Heard in a tribute which places Wells above Kipling.

Hillegas, Mark R. "Cosmic Pessimism in H. G. Wells's Scientific Romances," *Michigan Academy of Science, Arts, and Letters*, 1961. A valuable and clear study of the five major scientific romances as pessimistic evocations of T. H. Huxley's evolutionary fears.

James, Henry. *Notes on Novelists*. New York: Scribner's, 1914. This collection contains the essay, "The New Novel, 1914" (pp. 314–61) which led to Wells's vindictive parody of James in *Boon*.

Kauffmann, Stanley, "Wells and the New Generation: The Decline of a Leader of Youth," *College English*, I (April, 1940), 573–82. A sympathetic assessment of the decline of Wells's influence on the young.

Keun, Odette, "H. G. Wells—The Player," *Time and Tide*, XV (October 13, 20, and 27), pp. 1249–51, 1307–9, and 1346–48. There is savage invective here but also acute perception in this overwrought commentary of disenchantment by a once close friend.

Krutch, Joseph Wood, "Loss of Confidence," *American Scholar*, XXII (Spring, 1953), pp. 141–50. Wells and Shaw are viewed as representing the temper of their age. Krutch finds in the collapse of their hopes the end of those world hopes which they represented.

Maugham, W. Somerset, "Some Novelists I Have Known." *The Vagrant Mood*. New York: Doubleday & Co., 1953. Maugham concludes what is well known: that Wells died a disappointed man. The tone is affectionate, enlightening.

Maurois, André. *Prophets and Poets*. Translated by Hamish Miles. New York: Harper & Bros., 1935. An admiring humanist strikes at the heart of Wells's cosmogony. Wells's mistake, Maurois says, was to discount human frailty and fallibility.

Mencken, H. L. *Prejudices*. First Series. New York: Knopf, 1919. In "The Late Mr. Wells" (pp. 22–35), Mencken decries Wells's Messianic complex.

Nicholson, Norman. *H. G. Wells*. Denver: Alan Swallow, 1950. In less than one hundred pages, the author reveals in measured, never-hysterical tones how rich a literary vein Wells mined during his best period.

Orwell, George. *Collected Essays*. London: Secker & Warburg, 1946. Of all his allies, Orwell was the one Wells could least afford to lose. "Wells, Hitler and the World State" (pp. 160–66) details Orwell's conviction that Wells tragically lost touch with political reality in his misreading of the dangers of totalitarianism.

Orwell, George. *The Road to Wigan Pier*. London: Secker & Warburg, 1937. This compassionate book contains an early recognition of *When the Sleeper Wakes* and an excoriation of the tendency, attributed to Wells, to worship the Machine.

Pritchett, V. S. "The Scientific Romances." *The Living Novel*. New York: Reynal & Hitchcock, 1947. If not the most scholarly, certainly the most interesting, of a growing shelf of criticism which displays Wells's scientific romances as proof of the pessimism and anarchy which lay at the heart of his ebullient nature.

Salter, Sir Arthur. "H. G. Wells, Apostle of a World Society." *Personality in Politics*. London: Faber & Faber, 1947. Sympathetic and discriminating critique by a man who knew Wells well justifies the New York *Times* obituary leader on Wells which called him "the greatest public teacher of our time."

Schorer, Mark. "Technique as Discovery." *Forms of Modern Fiction.* Ed. William Van O'Connor. Minneapolis: University of Minnesota, 1948, (pp. 9–29). The essay holds up Wells's best novel, *Tono-Bungay,* to an arbitrary standard of excellence and finds it deficient.

Wagar, W. Warren. *H. G. Wells and the World State.* New Haven: Yale University, 1961. The best book yet written on the ideas and influence of Wells. Wagar examines all the charges brought against Wells and still concludes that, in the world society he sees as inevitable, there will always remain indelible traces of Wells.

————. *H. G. Wells: Journalism & Prophecy 1893–1946.* Boston: Houghton, Mifflin, 1965. Wagar's continuing effort to salvage Wells's dying reputation is little served by this exhaustive compilation of lesser works. Commentaries are invariably excellent.

Weeks, Robert P. "Wells Scholarship in Perspective." *English Fiction in Transition* (1880–1920). Published for the Modern Language Association Conference on English Fiction in Transition, Purdue University (Vol. III, 1960). An exemplary roundup of recent scholarship on Wells.

West, Anthony, "H. G. Wells," *Encounter,* VIII (1957), (pp. 52–59) and "The Dark World of H. G. Wells," *Harper's,* CCXIV (May, 1957), (pp. 68–73). West examines the entire tapestry of his father's works to point out convincingly that pessimism, not optimism, was in the true grain of his thought. The first essay is the fuller treatment.

Wilson, Colin. *The Strength to Dream: Literature and the Imagination.* Boston: Houghton Mifflin, 1962. Useful for its unorthodox view of Wells as a victim of the denial of existential aspects in men.

Wilson, Harris, ed. *Arnold Bennett and H. G. Wells.* Urbana: University of Illinois, 1960. These letters are most valuable in showing how common origins between two writers could cement a friendship.

Woolf, Virginia, "Mr. Bennett and Mrs. Brown." *Reading I've Liked* ed. Clifton Fadiman. New York: Simon & Schuster, 1941. This essay, almost self-effacing in its modesty, ranks with the most effective demolishments of the kind of novel written by Wells, Bennett and Galsworthy.

4. Miscellaneous

I can do no more than make note of the wealth of books and articles by some of Wells's peers—people like Sir Ernest Barker, Hilaire Belloc, G. K. Chesterton, Ford Madox Ford, Sir Richard Gregory, Frank Harris, Sir Julian Huxley, C. E. M. Joad, Harold Laski, Sinclair Lewis, Edward Marsh, Alfred Noyes, Lord Bertrand Russell, Bernard Shaw, Frank Swinnerton, Graham Wallas, and Beatrice and Sidney Webb.

Finally, I come to that list, again necessarily incomplete, of works of fiction in which H. G. Wells, or someone very like him, figures as a character. Wells acknowledged in his autobiography that he is Hypo Wilson in Dorothy Richardson's *The Tunnel,* which portrays the atmosphere at the soon-to-be-famous author's Worcester Park home (1896–97) with an accuracy Wells described as "astonishing." George Gissing describes a successful writer—nodding unmistakably at his good friend Wells—in *The Private Papers of Henry Ryecroft.* Max Town in Anthony West's novel *Heritage* (1955) closely resembles Wells in appearance, mannerisms, and outlook. West, the product of a union between Wells and Rebecca West, even has Town describe the writing of a story precisely like H. G. Wells's "The Cone." As Professor Wagar notes, Wells sometimes puts in a personal appearance in twentieth-century counter-Utopias: he is the "Prophet" in Victor Rousseau's *The Apostle of the Cylinder* (1918) and he is Horace Jules, the Director of the National Institute of Co-ordinated Experiments in C. S. Lewis's *That Hideous Strength* (1946).

Index

Index

Vallentin, Antonina, 123, 142, 144
Veblen, Thorstein, 94
Verne, Jules, 32, 46, 47, 48, 49, 90, 155n35
Victoria and Victorianism, 7, 26, 64, 66, 76, 77, 81, 88, 92, 101, 125, 134, 147, 150
Voltaire, 19, 126

Wagar, W. Warren, 58, 115, 122, 124, 127, 130, 147, 173
Walden (Thoreau), 94
Wallas, Graham, 130
Walpole, Hugh, 102
Ward, Mrs. Humphrey, 72, 87, 101, 103
Way of All Flesh (Butler), 76
Webbs, Beatrice and Sidney, 73, 85, 90, 103, 117, 138, 158n4
Weeks, Robert P., 146, 150, 164n7
Welles, Orson, 25, 31, 43
Wells, Amy Catherine (Jane), second wife of H. G. Wells, 17, 86, 89, 93, 99, 127, 135 (See also Wells, H. G., on Marriage)
Wells, Frank, brother of H. G. Wells, 54
Wells, G. P., son of H. G. Wells, 133
Wells, H. G.: Life and Times, 17–23; boyhood, 17–21; science student, 21–23; the early writer, 24–27; forebodings of, 28–29, 49; scientific romances, 30–50; short stories, 51–63; comic novels, 64–71; crisis and *Tono-Bungay*, 72–83; socialist and feminist, 84–96; conflict with Henry James, 72, 77–78, 97–105; novel of ideas, 97–112; World State and utopias,
86, 94, 113–32; educator, 132–135; despair and old age, 135–146; final assessment, 147–50; aerial forecasts, 52, 76, 115; angry young man, 64, 73, 103–4; anti-utopian, 22, 28, 61, 113, 117–18, 125; as Byronic hero, 84; conflicts of persona, 26, 58, 65, 66, 76; critics, 22, 97–105, 112, 115–16, 124, 128–31; existential aspects, 85–86, 120, 135–37, 145–46; historian, 98, 125–31, 133; income of, 58, 98, 109; influence of, 24–29, summary, 147–50; journalism of, 28, 76, 97, 105, 127, 138, 144; love scenes in novels of, 77–79; on marriage and sex, 58, 64–71, 78–79, 86, 88–96, 135; myth-allegory, 24, 35–39, 41, 54–63, 149–50; on novel-writing, 75, 99–105, 143–144; as prophet, general assessment, 147; on spirit of advertising and public relations, 79–81, 148; tank warfare, 52

WRITINGS OF:

Ann Veronica, 89, 91–94, 100, 103
Anticipations, 116–18, 147
Apropos of Dolores, 67, 95, 96, 136
"Argonauts of the Air" (story), 52
Autocracy of Mr. Parham, 141
Babes in the Darkling Wood, 89, 90, 101, 142–44, 146
"Beautiful Suit" (story), 57–58
Boon, 103–5
Brynhild, 136
Chronic Argonauts, 113